Tears Run Dry

A Story of Courage in the face of Poverty,

Tribalism and Racism

By Patrick Kalenzi

With Aliser Geiser

In loving memory of Baaba, my grandfather, the

indomitable gentle force without whose nurturing I would

never have become the person I am today.

One

February, 1980 (Baale, Uganda)

Kiboko *(cane)*

"Hey Long Nose! Homeless Tutsi... Got a name?" When I turned to answer, he held his nose between forefinger and thumb. "Wait, don't come over here, you smell of rotten milk!"

"I don't smell," I insisted, my voice drowning in my chest.

"Go home and bathe," he shouted, causing thunderous laughter from his posse. They fell into a chant of *Kanyarwanda,* "little Rwandese," and *Ensiyaleta,* "wanderer without a country," repeating the derogatory words over and over in an off-key ballad. He sauntered along at the head of a large group of older boys, pushing and sparring playfully. He was taller than the rest, with a hard square face that was impenetrably dark except for flashes of long white teeth and eyes lit by a cruel gleam. To my dismay, the intimidating group was heading my way.

I should have run as the mob of older boys closed in, but pride gripped my heart. Though my disadvantages in the situation were glaring, I couldn't still my tongue. "I despise your big crooked teeth!" I retorted. Muwonge charged.

For a minute he blocked the sun, becoming a shadow over me. Then, his giant hands lifted me off the ground, as if I too were nothing but a shadow, and flung me into the brick wall of my new school.

The angry shadow darkened and spread until there was nothing. No pain, no sound, not even my thoughts.

*   *   *

The day started well enough with a voice calling, "Patrick,

time to go to school!" School?

The last word jolted me awake so fast I nearly collided with the dim plastic flashlight my older sister, Joyce, held inches from my nose.

Satisfied with my apparent wakefulness, she disappeared with a quiet swoosh, her departure marked only by the dry clatter of the door of our two-room hut and the return of pre-dawn darkness. There was silence again, cut only by the sawing of crickets. I waited for my eyes to adjust to the moonlight slipping in through the window. Just as I set my feet to the floor, the door clattered again.

"Patrick!" This time, it was the round silhouette and persistent voice of my cousin Rosette as she fluttered at the threshold.

"Get up and get ready," she insisted. "You do not want to be late for your first day at school, do you?"

"Maybe he wants *Kiboko,* the Cane! Let's leave him." Joyce's voice trickled in past Rosette's nervous form.

At twelve, Rosette was the senior of the three of us, and the only one who had attended school. However, she'd prepared my sister Joyce and me well with stories of the many punishments administered to those who dared arrive late. The image of a tall teacher with crooked teeth and mean eyes, chasing after me with a *kiboko*—well-smoothed by the many kids it had been used on— pricked my scalp and chased off any lingering dreams. Besides, I didn't have to go gather the cows this morning! Instead, I was going to begin my education.

"Ok, you see, I am up!" I said, pushing myself from the bed. I flapped my arms at them and stumbled across the hard-packed dirt floor towards the door and the relative dawn promising itself at the forest's edges surrounding our homestead. The fresh-burning smell of my father's pipe hung in the air, but I could not make him out.

Dew-frosted grass tickled my feet as I trotted to the kitchen, a separate grass-thatched mud hut twenty feet from the main hut. The chilly breeze that followed me made off with the familiar smell of my father and I had a fleeting wish for more clothing for what promised to be a long hike through the jungle to school. I was only eight years old, but I'd already learned that wishing seldom did any good. I either had to do something, or put the wish out of my mind. And today, I was already wearing my warmest clothes.

In the kitchen I gulped down a little milk for breakfast while Rosette buzzed nearby. "Do you have your milk bottle ready?" she asked, tugging at the seams of her green polyester dress. It was a few sizes too small for her plump frame, and it cut into the soft skin of her arms.

"Milk bottle? For what? Aren't we staying there for only half a day?" I replied, lovingly squeezing my new notebook into the ochre cotton sac my mother had made me just for this occasion. She'd sewn its long straps extra thick so that they wouldn't chafe too much when I swung it across my chest for the three-kilometer trek to school.

"First of all, it is a full day and a far walk; we will

not be back until nightfall. Second, Mama said we should

all take something to eat or drink. Tell Joyce too," my

cousin instructed, waving her arms like a baby hoot owl. I

thought if she got any more excited she might fly away.

"Joyce!" she called into the grey morning. "Don't forget

your milk bottle!"

Though technically our cousin, Rosette had acted

the part of oldest child in our family ever since I could

remember. When she was four, both of her parents died of

a simple and easily treatable infection, and she became

another orphan of Uganda's poor medical system. My

parents took her in. Joyce was five at the time, and I was

barely a year old. In Uganda, Rosette's situation was all too

common; many children lost their parents to disease or

violence, and were raised instead by aunts and uncles. The

whole family treated her as if she were our sibling.

"I am not joking; you will be crying from hunger by

noon," Rosette warned.

"But I thought school serves meals," I said. Visions of cassava steaming from banana-leaf wrappers and cups of thick, milky *chai* brought a rumble to my empty stomach.

"No, dummy! They don't," she corrected simply, her arms flapping in frustration.

"I have my milk," Joyce called in her tinkling version of a shout as she popped up next to Rosette and me. "But wait, it's cold; I need a sweater."

"You both will make us late," Rosette scolded, wringing her hands in frustration. "You are tempting *Kiboko* for all of us." She made as if to start off towards the path to Baale town; a cold wash of fear filled my throat at the thought of being left to walk the dark jungle path to school alone. I rushed to the kitchen, where I found a half-bottle of milk my mother had prepared for me the night before, then sprinted to catch up, my bare feet sinking into the manure-thick mud, the tender young grass pulling up between my toes. "Wait!' I yelled. "I'll be lost!"

Nyabwangu, our faithful dog, bounded happily beside me, seemingly unaware that, either in school or in the jungle-bound pathway, there were things to be worried about.

"Not so fast!" A booming voice brought us all to a sudden stop. It was my father. His deep commands belied a slight build and short stature. When he scowled, the slick mass of black hair covering his head like a military helmet seemed to slide down and darken the scars on his forehead. We straightened our posture and lowered our eyes. Dada did not tolerate indiscipline.

"What are you doing with the dog?" he asked.

"The dog? Ahhh . . .," I muttered, searching my mind for an answer that I knew did not exist. Once my father had decided that we were disobeying, there was no convincing him otherwise. That is, unless you were my mother. And she was nowhere to be seen.

Dada closed in on us, his gaze suspicious. Behind

him, the sun began to push the clouds apart with its red glow. Time slowed to a sloth's crawl as we awaited the impending lecture. My need not to be late for school became urgent. Visions of the cane loomed.

"Dogs do not attend school," he declared. I studied the dark mud between my toes. By some miracle, Dada stopped there. He left us with a stern look and walked back towards the pastures.

My sister and cousin looked at each other, then at me. They were waiting for me to command the dog. I gave her a pat, comforted by the feel of her coarse fur, then, with a sigh, sent her home. "*Nyabwango, subiramurugo.*" Tail hanging low, she reluctantly padded back to the veranda where she liked to spend her days napping. As she retreated, she paused to cast a worried glance back at us, as if to let us know that, should we change our minds, she'd be by our sides in a flash.

*   *   *

The dark of the jungle closed around us quickly. Oaks dwarfed the leafy fig tree canopies. Intertwining Apples of Sodom, heavy with their poisonous fruit and fearsome thorns, twisted into a cruel undergrowth. The soft dirt path seldom saw more than foot traffic, it faded here and there where the brushwood snuck across with vigorous green tendrils. Tales spread by children in the village of a forest witch stiffened my spine. Time seemed to stretch longer as we worked our way deeper into the jungle.

"School is farther than I realized," Joyce muttered. I was almost glad to hear the quiver in her voice and know that she too was nervous. We were walking so close to Rosette, we nearly bumped into her every time she avoided a brush or dodged one of the pond-sized puddles blocking the road. Our cousin discretely maintained her motherly air and seemed to puff out to protect us.

Above our heads, a family of monkeys swung between the trees, their chatter kept close by the blanket of foliage above. Branches creaked, leaves whispered. And then, nearby, a loud rustle and the distinct sound of snapping wood.

"Did you hear that?" I asked.

"Hear what?" Joyce responded, as we all halted.

"That sound," I whispered, pointing. "Over there!"

As if on cue, a warthog with long tusks burst out of the underbrush and darted across the road in front of us to quickly disappear in the thicket on the other side.

"Eeeh, that was just a forest pig!" Rosette laughed as Joyce and I released her dress from cramp-knuckled fists.

We walked in silence for a while. Then, without warning, an antelope broke through the brush bounding straight at us.

I barely had time to let out a screech as I spun on my heel to sprint in the opposite direction. Joyce and Rosette were right behind me. We ran together for a few feet before I felt a hand grabbing at my shoulder.

"Patrick, slow down! That was just an antelope. They do not eat people, fool!" Rosette exclaimed.

"Then why are you running?" I gasped, allowing her to pull me to a stop.

"Because you idiots sprinted off so fast I thought maybe it was something to worry about; now I recognize it's just a stupid antelope."

"It was charging us! It had horns," I explained, my speech interrupted by the need to breathe. I bent down, hands on my knees, and waited for my heart to stop somersaulting.

The path wound infinitely deeper into the forest. It seemed that every time I had recovered from one scare there was another—monkeys, parrots, an ominous screech that was surely the witch.

Master Reuben

After what seemed a dark lifetime, the trail widened into a dirt road, and the jungle gave way to friendly gardens where plants grew in orderly rows. Huts sprang up here and there. As we walked further into the village of Misanga, other kids appeared from the shadows between ever-closer homes to fall in beside us.

Soon, a large building came into view. Its grass-thatched roof glinted hints of gold. It looked particularly stately and well-built. In front of the hut was a giant oak tree, the ground beneath it stomped hard and nearly free of grass. Children milled in its shade, trickling out into the golden daybreak light. The fear that had been souring my belly turned to excitement. I knew this was our destination.

Rosette took my hand and we entered the school grounds.

The door to Mr. Reuben's Village School loomed over me, the cut-out windows heralding in rays of light that cast harsh yellow shadows across the rows of wooden benches. A mass of identically-dressed kids milled around the room, pushing against each other, stifling giggles, their chatter a din within the thick brick walls. I looked down at my own uniform, and though it was the same as that of all the other boys—a collared blue shirt and khaki shorts made of rough cotton—mine was more faded and sac-like. While they formed a vibrant cohesive mass, I was shrinking into my garment and fading into the dull brown of the walls and the packed-dirt floor.

"DING DONG," The banging of heavy brass bell killed my contemplation and the air around me stilled as the seething mass became rows of still faces with eyes fixed on the front of the room. Joyce and Rosette had disappeared among them. I shuffled quickly to squeeze onto a bench and found a small space beside an older boy with long arms. There was a generous breadth of room around him, but instead of moving over, he looked at me with a mean snarl. I balanced on the edge of the seat so as not to brush against him.

At the front of the room sat the headmaster, reflecting back the silence until it sat so heavily in the room I held my breath for fear of being the one to break it. Mr. Reuben's long legs and arms were crossed. He surveyed us from a bench just a little thicker and taller than the ones we sat on. The old man's tight khaki uniform accentuated his wiry frame, and though there were many fine wrinkles in his light brown skin, and a definitive sharpness of his age-sunken cheeks, nothing about him suggested frailty. I was sure that when he opened his mouth words would fly out like arrows of knowledge to lodge themselves in my eager mind.

Instead of arrows, a song came from Mr. Rueben's mouth, and the whole room soon filled with the high, wavering voices of the children around me. All of them knew the words to our school's anthem.

After submitting to a quick inspection of combed hair, teeth, oral hygiene, lice, dirty shorts and body odors, a process that made me feel rather like one of our cattle, I filed outside with the rest of the new students to assemble for class under the matriarch oak. Joyce reappeared beside me, grabbing my hand, and I immediately set into chatting with such unrestrained excitement that I barely noticed she was more nervous than anything.

Despite the distractions of our outdoor classroom, I focused on that first lesson with a stern determination. This was not without challenge. Only a wall of bushes on one side and a garden of cassava and banana on the other separated the school property from the bustle of the village—the bellows of humans and livestock alike carried through the living fence. Those sounds soon faded into the background, but tuning out the antics of the flock of wild parakeets that shared our shade-defined classroom proved more of a challenge. They flew in and out, chattered in the branches, and dropped bits of sticks and straw on us as they worked on their nests. Their hatchlings were in incessant twittering for food and attention. A splatter of white droppings caused the whole group to erupt in squeals and laughter that the headmaster tolerated for a few seconds before calling us to attention again with a sharp command. If my focus was immovable, that of my classmates was not, and even on that first day I felt a creeping of frustration that my fellow students could not keep their minds on their tasks.

*   *   *

The first half of the school day vanished in a flurry of feathers and rising damp heat creeping in past the shade of our leafy ceiling. At lunch break, Rosette joined my sister and me. We hovered at a corner of the group, sipping our milk and digging furrows in the damp earth with our toes.

Rosette shared old gossip about the children who had attended school with her the year before. Her eyes narrowed as she nodded subtly in the direction of the older boy who had snarled at me earlier in the day.

"I don't want to scare you, but be careful with the tall boy in that group. Try not to talk to him. If you must, don't disagree or argue."

"Too late," I said. "What's his name?"

"Muwonge, but I call him *Rupfu*, the devil. I am serious, Patrick, be careful. Other students will ignore us for being Rwandese; he will do much worse."

Muwonge was closing in on us, and as Rosette whispered these last words he pulled to a stop and held his hand up to stop the throng of boys behind him.

"Let's run to the class," Rosette said, pulling at my shirt. As if to agree, the bell clanged, lunch break was over.

"I will not let him chase me off," I declared. Joyce shook her head at me as she and Rosette sprinted back to the schoolhouse. I turned to walk after them, but it was too late.

"Why is it that all Tutsis work with cows?" Muwonge spat, smirking at my bare feet. His were clad in rubber flip flops andwere much cleaner than mine, which were perpetually stained with dirt and manure. Clearly, he lived in the village and did not tend to cattle every morning or walk miles through the jungle to get to school.

"Because . . . because it is our tradition," I replied, drawing back my shoulders to try to seem big. He towered a full head over me, rendering it a rather useless task.

"My parents tell me you came to our country to be our slaves. Maybe they will let you work for us, and then perhaps you can afford a pair of shoes." Most of the kids at school did not wear shoes, Tutsi or not, but this fact did not soften his insult. Anger welled in me, and despite Rosette's warnings I found myself unable to keep it from escaping in my words.

"You are wrong!" I replied fiercely, refusing to back up as he stepped closer to me. "My family does not work for anyone. We own cattle and can afford whatever we need." Behind him, the other boys had stopped playing with a homemade soccer ball and gathered close.

"Your cow job, it makes you smell like their rotten milk. You smell like the ghee that your mother shakes out of the spoiled milk gourds," Muwonge retorted. He scrunched his nose and waved at the air by his face to indicate a terrible stink.

The sensation that this would end badly crept up my spine with prickly fingers. It seemed the bell had clanged hours ago and my gut turned with desire to be away from Muwonge and back in the safety of the classroom. But I couldn't let him have the last word.

"Keeping cattle is our tribe's tradition," I repeated proudly, thrusting my chin in the air. "And I work hard like any other Tutsi." With that I turned and walked as quickly as I could without seeming hurried back towards school. I didn't have to look to know that an angry mob of kids followed in my tracks.

Before I disappeared into the sanctuary of the school's eves, I heard Muwonge's voice again. It caused the hair on the back of my neck to rise. "Hey long nose!"

*   *   *

Comets of light began faint explosions in the corners of my eyes. A tap on my shoulder reminded me I had a body, the voice that followed brought my mind swimming back into the present.

"What are you doing here?" it inquired through the still-exploding blackness. "Get up and go to class, break time is over."

It wasn't until I opened my eyes to see where the voice came from that I realized they had been squeezed shut. A red badge blurred into focus: it was the school head boy, bending over me with irritation and little else. I skimmed the schoolyard as I dusted myself off. Muwonge stood in a corner, laughing to his friends as he pantomimed a reenactment of my beating.

My skin was bruised; an apple-sized knot swelled on the back of my head. But I felt no pain while Muwonge's taunts still rang in my head. Instead, creeping anxiety trembled my lips as I wondered if they could hold any truth.

They were so muchbigger and stronger than I, and their clothes fit on their bodies rather than hanging off them. Instead of being caked in manure, their feet were clad in sandals. While the natives filled the village, my peoplewere pushed to the outskirts with our cattle and their clinging dung.

Our trek home from school began in weighted silence. A shadow clouded Rosette's face, and even as she ushered us away from the school grounds, her body closed in on itself, as if she was a turtle trying to tuck into its shell. Except, Rosette had no shell. We had scarcely left the crowds of children released, laughing into the afternoon sun when her tears broke through. "Some girl called me a soft piece of cow ghee and pushed me," she sobbed. "I stumbled to the ground and all the other girls laughed."

"Please don't cry," I told her, discretely glancing around to make sure that Muwonge wasn't following us. "You can't let them think you are weak. It will only make things worse." It was the first time I had spoken since my own incident, and I realized I had a painful swollen lip. I tasted blood in my mouth as the split skin reopened.

Joyce eyed me as she put a consoling arm around our cousin. "Shush Patrick. Rosette is hurt. And instead of consoling her, you are telling her nonsense. What happened to your lip?"

I ignored the question. "We can't let these bullies

push us around just because we are Rwandese."

"Oh really? Well, how about because there are thirty of them and three of us? Or because you are half the size of the other boys! And maybe you should not tell Rosette what to do, but instead ask her for advice, because she is older and has been to school before." Joyce spat. Rosette was still shaking with sobs, a collapsed green polyester turtle with no shell, just her skinny cousins to shield her. I searched for a reply but found that my mouth was empty and tasted of blood.

Pride and disgrace battled inside me, making my stomach churn. I could not stop trembling. What would I do when the school day ended? Would I grab my sisters and run home? There was no way I could defend myself against Muwonge and his pack. They were a heavy thorny mass of sharp elbows and shaper words; I was more or less that lone strand of dry grass blown off the thatched roof by the evening breeze. As the school day slipped by, I wished for the wind to carry me and my troubles away.

Two

February, 1980 (Baale, Uganda)

Ibyansi (Calabashes)

We had been trudging for less than a kilometer when the first bolt of lightning lit the shady jungle around us. Thunder followed closely behind, snapping through the clouds to bring a waterfall of rain. We ran into the shelter of a tree so terraced with branches laden with broad leaves that its trunk remained dry even in the tropical downpour. Pressed together, shivering as the wind cooled our soaked bodies, we watched our trail transform into a muddy river.

After several minutes Rosette took a deep breath and declared, "We need to keep going. Otherwise, we're going to freeze." Straightening a little, she pulled my sister and me forward into the downpour. The bullies at school may have left her helpless, but here was a situation she knew how to handle.

Leaves and twigs whipped our bodies as we leaned into the gusting wind. Though we pushed on as fast as we could, it seemed we only inched forward. The mud and water brought pain and then numbness to our bare feet. I lagged behind, searching the sides of the road for another tree to hide beneath.

"What are you doing? Keep walking," Rosette urged.

"I have a speck in my eye, and I can't breathe well - the wind is heavy," I cried.

Shaking her head, she turned back and grabbed my hand.

"Come on Patrick," she said, her voice both gentle and urgent. "We still have hours to walk, and we'll be lucky to make it home before nightfall. I know it's uncomfortable, but unless we want to sleep out here, we must push on."

Barely a minute had passed when Rosette let go of Joyce and me to dash off towards a stand of banana plants just off the trail. She returned with three long, wide leaves.

"Use it like an umbrella," she advised, as she handed one to each of us. The leaf hung over my head, keeping the rain out and a little of my body heat in.

"This is much better," I said, smiling at her a little from under my green shelter. Rosette smiled back, and led us on towards home.

*   *   *

By the time we finally arrived home, the storm had slackened and the darkness of its clouds was replaced by that of encroaching night. I hurriedly changed out of my school uniform and went out to gather our small herd of cattle for their evening milking. Going to school did not mean we got to skip our chores.

Tending to the herd was a big responsibility, and I took it seriously. Milk was not only a staple of our diet but our family's only means of income. The five cows that we owned provided just enough to keep us fed and clothed. There was little leeway for mistakes.

As I approached the cooking hut with two warm, foamy pails of fresh milk, the fragrance of beans, ghee, onions and curry powder greeted me. It had been hours and miles since my last meal—the half-bottle of milk I'd had for lunch--and my stomach let out a decisive growl.

"Do you smell fried beans? I asked Joyce, who brushed passed me through the doorway.

"I know! I wish it was chicken, though. Trekking to school was hard work," she replied.

I smiled. We both knew that meat was a luxury for special occasions, and though the first day of school had been an occasion for us, it would not qualify. But it was still fun to dream about such things.

My mother, Florence, looked up from the clay pot she was stirring when we entered the kitchen. "I heard you two talking about chicken," she chided. "Don't be greedy. I am making a tasty meal. Be thankful for what we have."

I stole a moment to enjoy the warmth of the hut and its scents while my mother portioned half the milk into *calabashes*, the dried pumpkin-like gourds we drank from. Beads of sweat sparkled like dew on her straight, elegant nose, and her mass of mahogany hair gleamed richly inthe candle light. She moved about the hut on silent feet, and though she was a lithe woman, her character and strength made her seem much larger. She filled the room with a sense of warmth and safety. When she smiled, her long lashes and white teeth flashed, and wrinkles formed in the corners of her deep black eyes.

With one more rumble from my stomach, I sighed, left the warmth of the hut and headed back out to the *kraal*, the circular, split-log fenced enclosure where I milked the cows. Before dinner, they needed to be returned to the pasture to graze.

The rain had turned the *kraal* to a stinking soup of mud and dung. There was no avoiding the slop as I gathered the heard with clucks and gentle flicks of a switch. Though wading into the wet grasses of the pasture cleaned the debris off my feet and legs, I still sat down with a pail of water to scrub before joining the family for dinner. Until the exchange at school that day with Muwonge, I hadn't thought too much about the dark stains of earth and manure that clung to the calluses of my feet, but now every speck stood out to me. I wanted it off.

*   *   *

My family of eight ate meals in the central room of our three-room house—the only room that we could all fit into at once. Cowhide mats covered the dirt floor at meal times.

Kerosene lamps cast a warm light that seemed bright when we came in from the darkness of the outside. The moon hid behind thick clouds that were a near permanent fixture of Uganda's rainy season.

I quickly found an open space and sank down to the floor. It had been hours since I'd sat down, and the bliss of exhaustion relief washed over me. Rosette tiptoed between us, passing out plates heaped with fried beans and cassava. With that first bite of food, all the miles, teasing and work of the day disappeared; life seemed perfect.

A growl issued from a corner of the room. "This is not warm enough, Florence," my father declared. He pushed his plate across the mat towards Rosette who, despite having just sat down, immediately sprang back to her feet. Though my mother prepared the meals, as the oldest girl in the family, it was my cousin's job to assist with the kitchen chores. It was not unusual for my father to complain at mealtimes, and the responsibility fell on her to reheat his food, augment it with ghee or salt, whatever it was he called for.

My mother sighed and rose to her feet. She placed a hand on Rosette's shoulder, pushing her gently back to the mat and taking the plate out of her hands. "I'll get it," she said. Her eyes bored into those of her husband as she continued. "You've had a long day, beginning school again, not to mention taking such care with Patrick and Joyce, and being so responsible in completing all your chores as well." Her gaze and tone suggested that perhaps her husband had not done as much, but her words did not incite conflict. Lounging in stubborn silence, Dada took a long pull from his glass of *waragi*, local alcohol.

Florence spun towards the door and opened it without a squeak. Her wrap-around skirt swept the ground, whispering out behind her like a cool breeze.

*   *   *

My mother had just returned with the reheated food when

rain began to pound the roof again. Fat drops formed above me and dripped off the reeds and onto my head. I picked up my plate to find a dryer spot. As I squeezed towards a small space left between Joyce and a small table, I stumbled over someone's legs. Without thinking, I reached my free hand out to stop my fall, grabbing onto the table and nearly upsetting the kerosene lamp. Joyce screeched and lunged, snagging the lamp just before it sloshed oil on my bare arms and the curtains covering the wall behind it.

"Patrick, you klutz, what are you doing!" she yelled. The candle sputtered out. "I should buy a safe lantern one of these days; all these clumsy kids can't learn not to knock lamps over," my father grumbled from the darkness. Though he sat closest to the matches, he made no move to retrieve them. I heard my mother reach over him and grab the box. We all sat still, not wanting to upset the plates or each other in the darkness. Then, the crack of a match, and a glow lit my mother's still face. She shielded the flame with one hand and made her way carefully over to relight the lamp.

My father's appetite seemed to disappear with the light.He pushed aside the half-finished plate of food and retreated to his wooden chair. He snuggled in the corner furthest from the door. We finished our meal without speaking as he sipped his gin. He fiddled with his transistor radio, chasing his favorite songs through the crackly AM stations, spinning the dials in disgust when they were replaced by ones whose politics he did not agree with. It seemed an impossible task to avoid those songs. As a result, static and frustration filled the air.

Three

May 1983 (Baale, Uganda)

Rwabagabo *(one who is audacious)*

At the age of two, I earned the nickname that would follow me into adulthood: "*Rwabagabo.*" My grandfather gave it to me the day my parents brought me home, the unlikely victor over a severe case of polio. It was a knockout: I emerged from coma, and then paralysis, as strong and determined as ever.

In the late 1970s, polio outbreaks were common in Uganda. Children are especially susceptible to this highly contagious virus, and thousands—including me—were infected. Though vaccines had been available since the 1950s, it would not be until the late 1980s that they became widely accessible to poorer Africans. Until then, most Ugandans who contracted the virus were either crippled or killed.

In its severe forms, polio advances quickly. My parents were well aware of the outbreak in our area. When I developed the high fever, lethargy, and vomiting typical of the disease, they acted quickly. As my illness progressed, they rushed me from one hospital to the next, seeking adequate treatment. It was only through bribes—made almost unmanageably expensive by our status as Rwandese refugees—that they were able to get me care at the Mulago Hospital in Kampala, the only local hospital with facilities to treat advanced stages of the disease. By the time I arrived, I was deep in a coma.

Through the duration of my sickness, my mother refused to leave me. She sat beside my hospital bed, praying, crying, and holding onto my small limp hand, as if by doing so she could transfer to me her strength. When, after my first week of unconsciousness, my father argued that my life support machine be shut off, she would not have it. She begged for more time, and he relented.

Two weeks passed. "Even if he wakes up," the nurses told her kindly, "he will be severely crippled for the rest of his life."

Faced with bleak reality of my future, my mother's hopes began to wane. She prepared to say goodbye. "One more night," she told the nurses. "Tomorrow, you may shut off the life support."

The next morning, I opened my eyes.

I was so weak and crippled that, though my parents allowed themselves a grasp of hope, they accepted that I would probably not survive. For days I teetered feverishly on the brink of consciousness. Expenses racked up, and I made no improvement. Frustrated with the hospital's second-rate service only granted to us at first-rate prices, Mama began investigating alternatives. She found a Rwandese healer in a village near our home, and the hospital discharged me immediately, sending me away without medications or instructions—just a regulation pair of weighted leg braces. The clunky apparatus seemed ridiculous even to carry, given my prone and useless state, but my parents took them regardless.

The hundred-and-twenty kilometer trip took them through the city of Kampala, back past our home, through the rainforest, and to a remote village beyond. Mama clutched my nearly lifeless body to her breast as she and my father moved between crowded commuter buses. They transferred to the bed of a truck transporting huge metal containers of milk, on which the driver kindly allowed my parents a ride. For the last stretch, my father pedaled us over rocky jungle trails on a borrowed bicycle, my body arranged carefully between him and my mother, held up only by their strength. The useless braces dangled behind, polio's sad flag.

By the time my parents arrived at the mud-and-grass-thatched hut of the healer, despair clung to them like fruit flies to rotting cassava. A wiry, middle-aged man stood waiting for them, leaning casually on the door jamb. Mama handed me over as if I were already dead. Loose as that of a man my grandpa's age, my skin hung like thin, dark silk off useless arms and legs. My body was nothing but skin, bones and a beating heart.

Smiling down at my mother with a twinkle of sympathetic humor in his eyes, the man received the frail offering in one hand. "Look at you two," he said. "So hopeless. This one is going to be just fine. He's going to help himself now. And in not too long he will be helping others." He gestured with my limp body and gave my mother a conspirator's smile and wink. "That includes all the rest of the kids you're going to have."

For the next month, my mother and I stayed with the healer. His care was ritualistic and mysterious, techniques developed over generations and generations. The people of the tribe he belonged to, the Bajiji, identified as healers and psychics. Because the Bajiji consider it their place in life to be of service to their communities, they never ask for money. Though a part of the rituals they perform sometimes involves donations—in my case, a chicken and a cow—it is a small expense compared to hospitals.

My treatment began early every morning. Upon rising, the Bajiji made small cuts in my temples and on the ankle and forearm of my paralyzed right side. Chanting, he'd take a bit of my blood out to his herb garden to call upon higher powers for their assistance. He'd return with special herbs to rub into my fresh cuts. Throughout the day, his chanting continued, accompanied by manipulations and massage. He fed me simple meals of milk and porridge until my body could finally regenerate a little muscle.

When my father returned to bring my mother and me home on the back of his bicycle, I was no longer a body supported helplessly between them. Though my right side still hung useless, I held on with one thin left hand.

"There he is," my grandfather greeted us, smiling toothily as we pulled into the family compound. "My Rwabagabo. Welcome home!"

*   *   *

"Rwabagabo! How was school? Did you stay out of trouble?"

On mild sunny afternoons, my grandfather, who rented property adjoining ours, always stopped by for a visit. I'd come around the final turn of the path from school and spot him sitting on an old three-legged stool outside our house, my mother beside him, making use of her hands to weave or peel cassava as they gossiped. (Nyabwangu would dash to welcome me back.) It never took him long to look up and see me coming. Despite his eighty years, his senses were keen. He'd lift a hand at me as I walked the final meters and, more often than not, draw me into the conversation.

"Hello, Baaba!" I called. "My only trouble is not having enough books to read!"

After my rough introduction to discrimination at school, I'd more or less eased into a pattern of avoiding Muwonge and the other bullies. Because I could not keep my tongue when confronted, I'd learned that it was best to just avoid them. I moved between classes as quickly as possible, had my lunch close to the school, where the eyes of the teachers and head boy provided a shielding. In the past three years, these tactics had served me well. They not only kept me out of trouble, but also kept me very focused at school, where I earned top marks.

Baaba smiled at me with a jowly grin that spread to his kind and always slightly mischievous eyes. "That's my Rwabagabo. You keep getting in that kind of trouble."

I hesitated in front of him, tracing a circle in the dirt

with a bare toe.

"Rwabagabo, you should continue with your work or your father will be upset," Baaba advised.

"I guess I was looking for an excuse to rest...." I sighed as I headed out to gather the herd. Sometime into my first year, father had decided that our family could not afford to have school taking away from his children's abilities to complete chores. I would get up long before the sun crowned the horizon to help corral, milk, and tend to the cattle, while my sisters rose early to make the long walk to the well to fetch water. After school, work resumed and lasted until dinner. I always enjoyed time with my wise old grandfather, but especially so when it also meant an opportunity to rest between the trek from school and chores.

"I was just telling your mother about a couple I have been counseling," Baaba announced. His wrinkled smile revealed where his big white teeth had once contrasted with his sepia skin.

My mother rolled her eyes and sighed. She didn't say anything, but shook her calabash more vigorously, the cultured milk inside churning into ghee. Though she seldom stopped Baaba from stealing me from my chores, she liked to make a show of disapproval.

"You would take good care of your mother if your father abandoned her, wouldn't you?" he asked me, seeming to change the subject completely. Florence shot him a look and shook the calabash even harder. I worried it might fly out of her hands.

"Of course!" I replied. Then the meaning of what he'd said registered. "But why are you asking me this?" I tried to hide the panic that sprang into my voice.

Baaba chuckled and rubbed calloused hands against equally rough blue pants. Though worn from many washings, the pants hung neatly down over feet strapped tightly into sandals sewn from used car tires. His shirt was worn but well cared for, and the mismatched buttons did not take away from his stately bearing. While weaker shoulders curved under the years and the troubles they'd brought, Baaba's remained broad and strong. The slight pouch of his belly showed that his work had served him well enough; grandpa owned some cattle to keep him well-fed and comfortable.

"Sit down for a minute and listen. This is as important as all your studies." He patted an empty wooden stool next to him.

"Last night, a young couple came to me seeking council. Both their parents died during the 1959 Rwandan genocide, so they come to me when they need advice."

"Like the rest of this village," my mother quipped.

Baaba gave an acquiescent nod. He rubbed his eyes and blinked up at the sun fleetingly. "The woman wants a divorce."

Shifting his gaze over to me he continued, "I feel

bad they are fighting each other instead of fighting the injustices in this pitiless country we migrated to. Just like my children, those two don't realize that we have only each other."

Mama shot him a hard glance.

He shrugged.

"So tell us why the wife wants to leave him, Baaba," Mama asked.

"Well, the man has taken a second wife. Now the first wife is feeling forsaken, neglected. To make matters worse, the two of them just don't get along. I am worried that they will hurt each other—or him." He paused to dab at his mouth with an old blue handkerchief. Shaking his head, he mused, "Some Rwandese men still believe they are superior to woman, and therefore should own more that one wife. Ridiculous!"

"Own? That is what you call it, Baaba?" Mama replied, raising her eyebrows as the calabashcontinued to slosh rhythmically.

"That is how most Rwandese men see it. I do not. I have always had one wife, and God knows for a long time," he said, laughing. Baaba paused to light his pipe and puffed a spinning cloud of smoke.

"Regardless, we have no time and energy to waste on this bickering. What is done is done. I think she should try to focus on her children. I worry about their kids, and those of the rest of these young Rwandese couples whose sense of family was lost when we were forced to leave our homes, our country, and our roots."

Baaba pointed at me with his pipe. "Rwabagabo, listen up, I am going to speak of our history. You must know your past if you want to shape your future."

He drew in another long puff and continued. "Beginning in the late 1800s, European colonialists poisoned the Rwandese with propaganda aimed at dividing us so they could rule us more easily and profit off our resources. They forced us to carry ID cards labeling us as "Hutu" or "Tutsi." And even while they turned neighbors and friends against each other, they forced us to labor for them, growing their coffee and other crops, whipping us when we did not produce enough, as if we were mules. We Rwandese should not have let them get so far. We should have banded together, Tutsi and Hutu, to fight the colonialists. But instead, we let them play us against each other, as if we were pieces in a *mweso* game. And we Tutsi, losing the game, fled. Now we can't return, so we are men without land. A man with no country is like a stray dog; it either has to be submissive or vicious to find food and shelter."

We sat in heavy silence as Baaba picked up a handkerchief, wiped the corners of his mouth and eyelids, and then the top of his head. He lifted his eyes to the north, gazing far off into the distance, as if hoping to catch a glimpse of his homeland through the thick jungle. "I should

51

have fought and died in my country. Now your generation must live on to endure this misery."

When Baaba returned his gaze to us, there was a change in his voice, as if he'd come back from a distant place. "I say we must fight, and not each other! Instead, we should fight discrimination. We should be creating a community in which our children are nurtured by traditions—instilled with pride and strength, so that we may one day have a home again."

My mother, who had set down the calabash, picked it up and began to shake it again. She turned to me with a gentle smile. "Rwabagabo. Practice your heritage. Go check on the cattle."

I nodded solemnly and trod off towards the paddock. Behind me, I heard the conversation between mama and Baaba swell again, accompanied by the gentle swoosh of milk becoming ghee.

*   *   *

Our herd of cattle had changed; it numbered about twenty, including one bull. During the day my father—or I, if it wasn't a school day—would drive them out to publicly-owned lands to graze. We'd stay with them all day, following the grass. Sometimes the public lands were overgrazed, and we paid private land-owners for the temporary use of their pastures.

Before sunset, we brought the cattle home and lead them into a fenced corral. Regardless of whether it was a school day, it was always my duty to round up the milking group, which consisted of seven cows and their calves. I'd bring them into a separate, smaller enclosure, the *kraal*. Though Tutsi tradition forbade women from working with cows, my sister or cousin would sometimes help by distracting the calf while I milked its mother.

Cows have four teats, each with its own milk-producing gland. My father taught me to always leave one not milked, so that the calf would have enough food to grow healthy and fast. Of course, the calf didn't know this when I was milking—it would just smell that sweet scent and want to nuzzle in for a snack.

Though the work could be dirty and strenuous, conversations with Baaba always gave me strength. Leaving my grandfather's history lecture that evening, I barely thought about my tired legs. I walked slowly, enjoying the sunset turning the patch of sky over our family property a rich gold, the puddles dappling the muddy night paddock, reflecting pearly shades. The beauty, combined with the weight of grandpa's words, stirred me with pride in carrying on the Tutsi tradition of working with cattle. Eventually, I wanted to do more for my people, but even now, as a boy, I took my responsibilities seriously. So when I noticed one of the milking cows was missing, I sprinted off to find my father.

It didn't take long. My father lounged under his favorite mulberry tree, watching the shadows stretch. The distinctive smell of *waragi* wafted from him—sweet and stinging in the air—I gulped while words tumbled from my mouth. "I can only find four cows! Ngabo, the white and fawn striped cow, is missing!"

Liquor dulled my father's gaze. He shrugged his shoulders and shook his head. "I know; that cow has been gone since morning," he explained. The chickens pecking at the dried mulberries around him seemed more concerned. "I went and searched all day but couldn't find her." His fingers twiddled an almost empty glass.

"Could she have been stolen?" I asked.

"If so, she'd be the second this month. I don't think we'd have any better chance of getting her back than the first." He sighed and stared into his glass. "But, I'll report it to the worthless local chiefs in the morning. Then, since we are immigrants, they can ask us for a bribe that is worth the value of the missing cow. And that will be that."

"But isn't there anything else we can do? If it is our

cow and someone has stolen it—can't we just take it back from them?"

Papa laughed and gave me a look that let me know how young I was. "Easy as that!" he shook his head and reached for the bottle of *waragi* to refill his glass. "Let's just hope the stupid old cow is in the wilderness and will come wandering back tomorrow."

*   *   *

At school the next day, I struggled to keep thoughts of the missing cow out of my mind. I knew our family could not afford to lose more of our herd—we were living day to day as it was. It seemed so wrong, our tribe being continuously forced to endure injustices without hope of recompense. The bullying I received at school paled in comparison to Baaba being chased out of his own country, or people thinking they could take our cows because we were Tutsi and therefore deserved no rights to personal property. There had to be a way to change the way people thought about us—but how? Stealing back the cow seemed as useless a gesture as fighting back against Muwonge and his gang. It might make me feel better for an instant, but it did not solve anything. It would probably only make things worse. What could I do?

"Kalenzi!" The cracking voice of the school head boy pulled me from my musing. I straightened up at my desk and looked around. All the other kids in class pretended to be studying, but I could feel them listening. The head boy looked down at me with a bit of irritation and wrinkled his nose. "Mr. Reuben wants to see you in his office."

*   *   *

A dilapidated text book, its pages yellowed and curling

with age, lay centered on Mr. Reuben's plain wooden desk.

"Morning, Patrick! Please sit down." He gestured to the chair squeezed between the door and his oversized desk, which took up most of the room. I sat down, my spine rigid. Two more books, bearing the same ink-faded title as the one before me, lay off to the side amidst chalk and paper. Mr. Reuben noticed my gaze and nodded towards the copy in front of me.

"This is a compilation of several condensed stories of well-known African legends," he began.

I shifted uneasily, wondering why he was telling me this. The lost cow trotted out of my mind.

"Go on, take a look."

The book felt fragile and heavy in my hands. On the faded and creased cover was a picture of an African man and woman. The man wore a cloak about his waist, and held a spear in his hand and a skinny, long-horned cow stood by his side. The woman was draped in a traditional dress woven of tree bark. Inside the book, tiny words pressed together closely, a magical jumble upon the page.

"I want you to read the story of Kintu and his wife, Nambi," Mr. Reuben said, marking the page.

I knew the story—a creation myth told by Uganda's Buganda tribe. According to this legend, Kintu was the first person on earth, the father of all people. But when I opened the page and saw all the words, I shook my head.

"This?" I looked up at Mr. Reuben, showing him the sheet, making sure we were on the same page.

He nodded.

"Now?"

Again, he nodded. Nervously, I traced the faintly raised words with my fingers. There was so much more black than white. And where were the pictures?

"I can read one sentence at a time, but this is more than I have ever seen on one page. I don't know that I can keep them in order!"

"Patrick, just give it a try," he said with a benign smile.

I nodded.

"Okay."

"But it seems to be a long story."

"Start from the first page."

Realizing I was going to have to try eventually, I took a deep breath, exhaled to calm my nerves and studied the first page.

"In the begging . . ."

"Stop! The word is beginning," Mr. Reuben corrected. "Don't be nervous, Patrick. You can do this. Try again."

Even though he asked calmly, wrinkles of frustration crept in around his narrowed eyes.

"Okay . . . In the be-gi-ning, there was one man named Kintu," I read, my lips trembling. "He lived with his cow that . . ." My speech slowed, unsure of the next word, my mind still in panic over whether I had pronounced the others correctly. I was too careful, too unsteady, fearing to fail, like the first time I rode a bicycle. At some point, you just need to get on and start pedaling.

"Patrick." Mr. Reuben said, putting a hand over the book. "Your math teacher says you have a good memory, and can add numbers fast. These words are like numbers. They add up to a meaning."

"Numbers? No, these are words!" I argued. "They are long and detached from each other with no specific end. With math, either you know the answer or you don't."

"Ha! That is correct, Patrick. But what about a story? It has a beginning, a middle—which is like the plus or minus sign—and an end, which is like the answer. It depends on how you see it." He pointed with his index finger at the book I held. "Here's what we are going to do. Take this book with you. Study Kintu's story, and be ready to recite it for the guests at next week's parent-teacher general assembly."

"But, Sir, I—"

Mr. Reuben interrupted my protest with an upraised finger.

"Two other students will also be reading from the story. It will be a competition of sorts. And here is what is special about that day: the county chief is coming to our school for the first time ever. This is our chance to impress him and win his favor. Be well prepared."

His words carried both warning and praise. Then, his eyes seemed to remember my trembling, and his voice softened. "If you have any questions, bring them to me. You are one of the school's best readers, Patrick, and you are a fast learner. You will be ready. Make the school and your family proud."

Inkoni *(stick)*

That evening, I hurried through my chores so I would have time to study. As the importance of this competition became clearer in my mind, determination pushed fear aside. All the troubles my family and tribe had seen were because of the derogatory notion that we Tutsis were dim-witted and undeserving of property, power, or even basic human rights! We might be too outnumbered to fight back physically, but that did not mean we had to give up. Here it was—a way for me to win respect for me, my family, my tribe, and for the other Rwandese kids at school.

I was so caught up in my thoughts that I barely noticed when Baaba appeared at the pasture fence.

"Rwabagabo! I thought your job was to milk the cows, not to become one," he called.

I looked down at myself, knee-deep in the silvery pasture, and wondered how long I had been standing there, lost in thought amid the peacefully grazing cows. A piece of grass hung from my lips.

"Oh! I was studying," I replied.

Baaba, illiterate and from an old tradition where history and knowledge were passed down in stories, nodded his acceptance of this explanation. He leaned against the wooden rail, thwacking it gently with his *inkoni*, as if to test its strength. In Tutsi tradition, Grandpa always carried his stick with him, but not to lean on. Despite his eighty years, he held it powerfully. The smooth knobby head was polished to a shine with ghee; the wood gleamed dark and strong. Some men carved intricate designs in their *inkoni*, but grandpa preferred his plain and practical. It was a symbol of masculine strength, and could be used to herd cattle, separate bulls, and fight off an attacker when necessary.

I wandered over to where Baaba stood to tell him about the reading contest. He smiled and swelled with pride as I spoke. "You must be well prepared! This is your chance to show these natives the strength and power of the Tutsi. Show them that even when they try to keep us down, even with all odds against us, we will not just survive, we will excel!"

He fell into a silent thoughtfor a minute, staring off down the road to Baale town. Then his eyes narrowed, and the smile disappeared from his face. Instinctively, he tossed the stick up in the air and it landed in his firm grip.

"Rwabagabo, look down the road—something is not right." He strained his aging eyes against the sun. I followed their gaze. Yes, something was not right at all.

"It's Dada—but he is—he is walking his bicycle instead of riding it, and he's not moving right," I said. I held my palm over my forehead to shield the blinding sunlight. Baaba had already begun walking towards his son. I jumped over the gate to follow him. Baaba's pace seemed unbearably slow, and I pushed ahead at a restrained trot, then a full-out run. I glanced back, saw that Mama had come out of the house and was closing in behind Grandpa. Her long traditional skirt tripped her as she ran.

I rushed past the dangling Apples of Sodom and through the narrow path, barely feeling the elephant grass that brushed at my arms. As Papa neared, the sun caught his face in a reddish shimmer. His left eye was swollen shut, his face tight with suffering.

"He is hurt. Go Rwabagabo, help him," Baaba gasped behind me, the urgency of his voice cutting through his need for air.

No words left Dada's mouth as I drew near, all his energy spent on pushing the bicycle towards home. For a moment, his eyes didn't even register me, and I thought he'd walk right by. Then, they met mine. I saw recognition cross his face, briefly, before he stumbled, the bicycle clattering down into the sun-gold grass. I lunged just in time to catch him. His body reeked of anger and alcohol. I staggered under the weight, the odor, and the sticky feel of his blood and sweat. Soon, Baaba arrived beside me, and slung one of Papa's arms over his shoulder. Supported now on both sides, he wilted against us, his head too heavy, his knees threatening to buckle.

A few steps away Mama came to a stop. It seemed as though pain clenched her stomach, for she held it with one hand and the other clasped her mouth, stifling a scream.

"It is blood, isn't it?" she managed to whisper before doubling over involuntarily, body heaving in a dry retch. For all her strength, Mama could never stand the sight of blood. If I scratched myself playing soccer, or got cut in a neighborhood brawl, she always called Dada or Grandpa to dress it. This was beyond her tolerance.

It was blood, and there seemed to be too much of it. Some of it had dried in Dada's hair. A gash across his temple continued to ooze over his face, neck and chest. His shirt was drenched in shades of red.

"What happened, John? What happened? Goodness, tell me," Mama cried, keeping her back turned to us.

My sisters, hearing the commotion, scampered out from the yard and started crying too. Their sobs mixed with the chirping crickets, singing birds, and groaning cattle to create an overwhelming cacophony.

"Be careful, son, watch your head," Grandpa said, his voice low and soothing, as we approached the doorway. The three of us could not fit through at once, so I withdrew and allowed Baaba to take all of his son's weight. He walked him carefully through to the ladder-back chair in the sitting room.

I rarely heard my grandfather refer to Dada as "son." My thoughts traveled back to what he'd said about family and tribe—that we only have each other. Baaba may not always approve of my father's choices and actions, but he would always be his father. Here we were, brought together by violence perpetrated against us. It was a time to remember that we were, now and always, family.

"Bring that block for his feet, Rwabagabo," Grandpa instructed.

Shock tunneled my vision, but I managed to pull out the wood block for my Dada's feet to rest on. The dark little room resounded with sobbing and screaming. My grandmother and Auntie Kamugudu, my father's sister, stood swaying, their palms cupping their mouths or the trembling bodies of my sisters and cousins.

"Joyce! Get me a clean cloth. And some water." Grandpa ordered, bent over his son. His grizzled old fingers gently prodded his forehead near a gaping wound, provoking a fresh trickle of blood. We helped my father slide out of his shirt, revealing dark bruises spreading across his torso.

Baaba took the rag from Joyce and began to dab at his head, cleaning off the wound before wrapping it tightly so that pressure would staunch the flow.

"It is the Hutus, isn't it?" Grandpa whispered, either to Dada or himself—I couldn't be sure.

Dada arched his right brow, but remained silent.

"Baaba," Mama hissed. With some of the blood gone, she had regained her ability to speak and was finally able to look at her husband. "You know very well that the district of Baale has never been home to Hutus or Tutsi."

"They are a stain on my mind," Baaba murmured. "Anyone who commits such immoral acts is no different than a Hutu." Dada winced as Baaba cleaned his wounds with more vigor.

"It was . . ." he murmured painfully. The room silenced at his low, rough voice—the first words he'd spoken. Only a few muffled sobs broke through from the youngest of my sisters. The older women shushed them.

Haltingly my father continued, "The Nyara tribe. It was the Nyara."

A still fell over the room. My siblings fell to the floor, into prayer. I did not move, thoughts flying back to the missing cow. Some weeks ago Grandpa had mentioned rumor of the Ugandan Nyara tribe stealing from Tutsi herds. We were no longer in Rwanda and therefore the thieves were not Hutus , but we were still Tutsi. And if my father had confronted them . . . images coalesced in my mind. My father, strong, but small—and only one man against perhaps many of them. The liquor on him, some spilled, some on his breath . . .

I could see Baaba's thoughts were traveling the same path. "You confronted them?"

Dada nodded his head weakly.

"About the cow?"

"Yes," Dada replied. "About both of them." He opened the eye that was not crusted shut with blood. It peered clear and sharp at grandpa.

"I found them at the station." Stations were

gathering places where locals would meet to gossip and drink *waragi* or the local sugar cane liquor. As immigrants were not welcome at them, my father certainly would not have received a warm reception by showing up and inquiring about missing cows. Baaba pressed a hand to his temple, as if the hopelessness of the situation gave him physical pain.

"I spent the entire morning searching the savannahs for my lost cow." Dada's speech slurred from his swollen lip and exhaustion. "The cattle rarely venture far into the jungle, but I scoured the edges that surrounded the swatches of rolling grassland, in case they had gotten caught in dense undergrowth. I went house to house, asking around the neighborhood. Then I sought out the local chiefs. They scoffed at me, offering nothing unless I wanted to offer a bribe worth more than the cow itself. By then, the day was waning. That's when I decided to go to the station, where I knew I would find more local men. Of course, they were drinking."

My father did not mention his own alcohol consumption, but his breath gave it away.

"Those Ugandan natives answered the way they always do, telling me I had no right to ask about the cow, if it was gone, then it was gone."

"See, that's the problem," Baaba said brusquely. "Many of the natives believe that immigrants—especially, we Tutsis—don't deserve any right to any property."

"Five members of the Nyara tribe attacked me," Dada said. "I had no one on my side."

Telling his story left Dada weakened, and he soon slipped into a silent, semi-conscious state. The cut on his forehead seeped blood. Baaba shook his head and worked his lips over empty gums while he inspected his son's injuries. The world wound in slow motion, my siblings in the corners, crying, my mother, hiding her face from the blood but unable to leave her husband's side, my aunts gently sobbing.

"He'll need to go to a hospital," Baaba murmured, and then his eyes fell on me.

"What should I do, Baaba?" I asked, desperate to help.

Baaba waved me off. "I will take care of this," he said firmly, his eyes boring into mine. "You have other things to attend to. Now go. Go study your story."

*　　　*　　　*

The next week sped by in a blur of activity. When I wasn't studying, I was taking on extra chores while my father recovered. Bruises marked his face and body, and fourteen jagged stitches crusted and dried across his forehead. He had been stitched without proper anesthetic, as a few months before the Ugandan government blocked all medical supplies from coming into Baale because a guerilla group was looting hospitals to treat battle casualties. Baaba supplied the poorly trained paramedics with an anesthetic herb, but even with that, Dada said the suturing hurt like a poisoned arrowhead being dragged through his flesh.

Rather than discourage me, these setbacks made me more determined than ever to impress the county chief and all the others who would be in the audience at the school's general assembly. Here was a way to avenge my father's injuries.

I read the ten-page story of Kintu from start to finish. I read it over and over again. I read when we walked to school, holding onto Rosette's sleeve so I wouldn't trip over things.

I readwhen I was grazing the cows. I woke up early before school to read, and I stayed up late, reading until the printed words were no longer necessary, and I could stand with the cattle, reciting the entire story in my head.

The day before the general assembly, all of the

students gathered to prepare the school grounds. We dusted benches and tables, cleaned moss, pulled cobwebs from the walls, and slashed the African couch grass covering the yards. We even aligned the pebbles that marked a circle at the center of the grounds. Within the circle, lilies and roses bloomed in bold shades of yellow and pink. The soccer field was mowed fresh, the goal posts erected with new straight poles, and the field lines restored with wet white ash.

*   *   *

The day of the contest was overcast, wet whistling winds blowing grey clouds low across the sky, trees hanging heavy, and puddles taking over the sodden earth around them. Anticipating the mud, I walked to school that morning in my regular clothes, carrying my uniform— khaki shorts and a blue shirt—in my canvas bag so that it would stay dry and clean. My father had surprised me with a new pair of shoes especially for today's event, and as I tried to get the mud off my feet at the entry to the schoolroom I contemplated what the best time would be to put them on. Just as I decided to start wearing them so as to adjust to walking in their awkward length, the head boy showed up over my shoulder, ordering me to Mr. Reuben's office.

I pushed open the thin screen of a door to find my two competitors standing attentively. Neither of them were friends of mine, and both, unlike me, were Ugandan natives. Steven, tall and reedy, was the more boisterous of the two, and though he'd never tormented me I had seen him eating lunch and playing soccer with Muwonge and the other bullies. The other boy, James, was short and chubby and stared out at the world with big, scared eyes. Like me, he kept to himself at school.

I filed in behind them, waiting for Mr. Reuben to

finish scribbling something in his notebook. He pushed it aside and arched an eyebrow.

When he stood to address us, I noted that he'd exchanged his regular uniform: a short sleeve-shirt, black pants, and sandals, for a more formal attire: a long-sleeved white shirt, brown pants with a frayed white belt, and a well-worn pair of brown leather shoes. The clothes gave him an official look. The seriousness of the impending event sent a chill up to my skull.

"This is how the contest will work: When the time comes, all of you, one at a time of course, will be brought on stage to read Kintu's story for the guests. Then a select group of voters will decide who reads best. The boy who wins the contest will receive the honor and responsibility of presenting this poem." Mr. Reuben's deep, dark eyes held the gaze of each of us as he handed out the worn, typed pages. Each copy bore the marks of a different life, dark smudges on the paper, a little tear at the corner, letters worn where fingers had traced them so many times, perhaps trying to find the meaning in them by feel when the words refused to reveal themselves otherwise. I wondered who else had held this poem, and whether his hands had clutched it as tightly as mine did now, only to smooth it out later, apologetically, while asking that it give up its secrets.

Those of us in the contest were excused from class that morning, and I spent my time beneath the huge oak in front of the school, where I had received my first lessons, studying the poem. I leaned my back against the huge trunk, the matronly tree protecting me from the rain with layers upon layers of thick grey branches bearing leaves as wide as my head. So well sheltered was I beneath its cover, and so intent upon the poem, that I didn't even notice when the clouds dried out, leaving behind bright calm skies. The guests who had begun to gather near our makeshift wooden stage folded away umbrellas; those who had covered their heads with large banana leaves tossed them aside.

The quiet left behind by the rain filled with chattering and rustling. Pulled from mymemorization, I took a moment to observe the audience. There were over fifty parents, as well as the county and sub-county chiefs, and education officials from the ministry. My eyes were drawn to a couple of local chiefs emerging from their van. Their polished shoes, bulging bellies, and slick suits made them look awkward among the lean, barefoot crowds clad in bright traditional fabrics.

Baaba and my father had spent enough time arguing with the political news that streamed through our crankshaft AM radio, that I was aware of the corruption of the Ugandan government, but this was the first time I actually saw it. According to my father and grandfather, these men were moral perverts who would embezzle funds meant for roads, schools, and hospitals, and ruthlessly demand bribes to perform services that taxes already paid them a salary to do. The stark contrast of their wealth to the humble situation and poverty of the people they served confirmed the gravity of corruption in my mind. For a brief moment, I lost hope that my reading of a poem or a story could actually affect these men at all. What was a poem, when what they cared about was cash, goats, cows, and other things of material value? What were a few words, bumbling from the lips of a skinny boy with dirt permanently staining every crack in his skin? What could they possibly do?

*   *   *

Steven read first. I wasn't listening to him, but to the thumping of my heart, to the thoughts racing through my mind. Standing nervously beside the stage to await my turn, I searched the crowd for my parents, for Baaba, allowing myself to hope that in spite of his old joints, he had miraculously come. I saw nothing but a sea of vague faces shifting in the still warm glow of day, beneath the din of twittering birds, buzzing insects and Steven's dissolving words.

Then, I was next. I climbed the two steps onto the stage. The makeshift podium, a high wooden table laid with a white cloth, loomed, official and intimidating, too clean and crisp for my hands and my dog-eared book, or anything else I might carry. It didn't hide me at all from the crowd, but framed me for their eyes to find me better. As gently as I could, I placed the book before me, my fingers shaking as I spread it open to the first page. I'd thought I wouldn't need the words anymore, that the book would be just for show, but the haze of faces before me threw a lead cloud over my mind; all of a sudden the story disappeared and I knew nothing but a cold wash of panic dripping over every inch of my skin. Sucking in air, I pulled my eyes from the kaleidoscoping crowd and let them rest on the familiar text before me. I began to read.

"In the beginning, there was one man named Kintu.

He lived with his cow that provided him with milk for food.

One day, Gulu, who was heaven, sent his servants, angels,

to bring Kintu's cow to him. Kintu had no option but to go

to Gulu and demand for his cow back.

Gulu, promised to give the cow back if Kintu could

pass several tests: One of those was to eat a lot of food,

locked up all alone. When he couldn't finish it all, ants

came and helped him finish the food.

Then, Gulu told Kintu to make fire out of rocks.

Before Kintu could tell Gulu that he couldn't perform such

a task, natural forces appeared to him and lit the rock

particles into flames.

After performing more such tasks, Gulu appreciated

Kintu's wisdom and sent him back to earth. Kintu asked to

take Gulu's daughter, Nambi, with him. Gulu accepted but

warned that they had to leave secretly before his estranged

son, Walumbe, the devil, returned from his hunting trip.

Gulu knew Walumbe would be a danger to them and their future offspring.

As Kintu and his wife Nambi left for earth, Nambi remembered she had forgotten her millet in heaven. She ran back to collect it. Walumbe had just returned from his hunting trip and he followed her back to earth! Since then, he has caused disease, death and misery for Kintu, his wife, and their children!

I knew the story was over only because the pages ended. Though time had seemed to stretch on forever, I could barely remember reading. As the audience clapped, I rushed from the stagemortified. Surely I had read too fast, forgotten punctuation, rhythm, perhaps even words. Surely the audience was only cheering to spare me complete embarrassment. My legs trembled and I felt a sudden desperate need to use the bathroom. Then, I saw Mama.

She stood at the very back of the audience, peeping over another woman's shoulders, trying to catch my eye.

Our gazes locked and she smiled broadly and made a subtle

wave. Fear washed away, pride straightened my spine.

Even if I did not win the contest, I had performed well

enough to make my mother smile. If I won I would not

miss the chance to show her—and everyone else—how

well I could read the short poem. The story was just a

warm-up. In moments, a deep desire to demonstrate my

skill pushed away my desire to flee. I continued to tremble,

but no longer with fear. Now, it was with eagerness to hear

my name announced as the winner.

*   *   *

When we'd all finished reading, the boys and I shuffled

nervously next to the stage, while the judges convened to

choose a winner. They were a stern-faced group, some of

the more respected and educated people in our village. I

tried without success to peek into their huddle as officials took over the podium to make announcements and encourage their constituents to vote in the next election. Time seemed to stretch, each minute feeling like a thorn slowly pulled from my skin.

Finally, Mr. Reuben took the stage. He stood calmly with a folded piece of paper in his hands, and the murmuring crowd turned silent. I watched him, but my hearing had cut off, as if I were underwater.

For a moment I forgot I was part of the contest. Leaving my place by the stage, I started to walk towards Mama. My new shoes made my feet awkwardly long, and they seemed to brush against the toes of every guest in the silent audience. I excused myself again and again, but their eyes scolded harshly.

"Our special guests, parents, teachers, and students, we have a winner of the contest," Mr. Reuben announced, his words barely trickling in to my consciousness. "This boy, a proud product of our school, shall present for you a special poem." Finally, a smile spread across his face as he slowly lifted his eyes from the page.

"And the winner of today's contest is . . . Patrick Kalenzi!" Just as I reached Mama, the applause, mixed with grumbles of protest, erupted from the audience.

"What are you doing?" Mama asked, excitedly pointing to the stage.

"What?" I replied, perplexed that she did not hug me or congratulate my reading.

"They called your name!" she said.

"They want me to read my story again?" I was confused, uncertain that I could possibly have won the contest, pitted against two older native boys, that it could possibly have been so easy, over so quickly.

"Patrick, you won! You've been chosen to read the poem." She gently slapped me on the shoulder and steered me around, back to the stage. "Go now, I will be right here. Make me proud."

Before pushing my way to the front I stopped for a last look back. Traditionally dressed Tutsi woman pulled me forward by the wrist and said, "Well done, son."

More guests around us began to turn and look. I ducked my head and made my way to the stage through a crowd that now parted before me. The chiefs, seated at the front of the room, nodded and smiled as I passed. Quietly, I ascended the two creaking wooden steps. Onstage, Mr. Reuben greeted me with his gap-toothed smile. He reached out and took one of my hands in both of his, shaking it warmly.

"Well done, Patrick," He said in a voice loud enough for everyone to hear. As a second round of applause began to ripple through the crowd, he leaned down to whisper, "It's your time to shine." Motioning me to the podium, he tipped his head respectfully, turning the stage over to me.

The audience quieted while my insides, especially

my heart, pounded louder. I wondered if they could hear the "thunk, thunk" or the strenuous sucking of breath. My lungs must have shrunk; I could not fill them with enough oxygen. For a second, a lifetime, I was empty again, a black void before the eyes haunting me like glowworms in a dark field. Then, I felt the text book where it had found kinship with my damp trembling grip, and through the grimy feel of its pages I once again became aware of my hand that held it lovingly all day, the arm that held that hand, the trembling body that anchored them all. I raised the book to the podium, opening it up to where I had tucked the poem into its pages, and raised my eyes from the book.

There was Mama, at the front of the audience, her palms held in front of her chest like the Virgin Mary. Joyce and Rosette stood proudly at her side. Calm washed over me. The proud straightness of their spines gave strength to my waning core and my lungs could fill again.

"Dear guests," I addressed the audience as Mr.

Reuben had instructed. "Thank you for coming today," I bowed deeply and closed the text book.

Concern flicked across Mr. Reuben's face. "It's okay, Patrick," he whispered to me, leaning so only I could hear. "You can read the poem," These last words came out as more of a command than reassurance.

"No, Mr. Reuben," I replied. "I do not need to read it. I have it stored in my mind."

Mr. Reuben scowled.

"It's like numbers, remember? You either know or you don't!" I reminded him, and then turned to face the crowd. Beside me, Mr. Reuben sighed. "Okay. Go on, son."

I allowed my gaze to pass over the entire audience, lingering on those of each chief. Quiet grew to fill the air. I took one last look at my family, filled my lungs with air, and began.

Tools that teach us to be great come from birth.

A son, a daughter; from a parent that toils to

nurture them.

We are tasked, the land is ours, and the thoughts are ours too!

Then, what do we do? What becomes of us when we falter?

Amidst trauma and tension—we will remember, we will regret, we will wonder!

Now, my fellow fathers, my dear mothers, my strong brothers, let's train them, be that it may take, bring what is tried!

It works when you teach them, teach them, teach them . . .

My last words fell into solemn silence. Then, a few bold claps echoed, joined by more, until the air vibrated with cheers, clapping and stomping. The crowd all rose to their feet, even the chiefs, and as I made my way down off the stage to join my family, the congratulatory words whirred around me, as warm hands patted my back and gripped my shoulders.

Behind me, Mr. Reuben had taken back the podium. Over the din of the audience, he boomed, "I hope that from this poem, you have learned the great potential every child possesses, a potential that can only be fulfilled when *you,* their parents, choose to educate them." The applause swelled again.

*   *   *

Two weeks later, Mr. Reuben informed me that my reading had such an effect on the local officials in attendance as to earn our school government aid for the first time in its history. This news fed in me the mixture of pride and the increasingly daunting sense of responsibility born of my victory on the stage. I had not only achieved a victory over Muwonge and the other racist bullies at school but, I had earned funding that would allow the continued education of all the children in my village. If I had the power to create this change simply by reading a story on a makeshift stage, what more could I do, must I do, to help liberate my family and my people from the oppressive rule of the Uganda Peoples' Congress, an anti-Tutsi regime?

Four

September, 1983(Baale, Uganda)

Bazungu *(white people)*

On the weekends, my days were again spent tending to our herd. Though the work could be physically hard, it also meant plenty of down time as the cattle grazed and slept. One afternoon, Dada and I lazed under our favorite mulberry tree near the house, slow and sleepy with our bellies full of cassava meal. We listened to the nation's independence celebrations on his transistor radio.

"Fellow citizens. Today, September ninth, 1983, we honor those who struggled with us and before us to secure our independence." It was a resounding voice, filled with patriotic rhetoric—the voice of Milton Obote, Uganda's President. In 1962, Obote led Uganda to independence after sixty-eight years of British colonial rule. I listened, feeling proud of my country. "Fellow citizens," the President repeated. "I want to assure you that we will defeat the bandits fighting our capable and mighty army."

I looked up to see Baaba coming towards us. His bronze skin glowing in the bright sun, he seemed to epitomize the physical description used to stereotype Tutsis. Though bent over with his years and relying heavily on his *inkoni*, his above-average height was still as apparent as his long nose and golden color.

The words of the president must have carried to Grandpa as he crossed the field; he arrived visibly irritated and muttered a *Muraho*greeting as he settled himself on a stool beside where Dada and I lay with our backs against the tree.

"That rubbish he's saying is not for us," He said, waving a dismissive hand at the radio and spitting in disgust. "We don't belong here—we are not from here."

Suddenly, I did not feel as patriotic.

"The Uganda Peoples' Congress, the UPC, is grooming the youth wing for tomorrow's leadership," the radio continued.

"Not tomorrow's leaders, Mr. President," Baaba yelled at the radio. "You might as well call the UPC tomorrow's murderers!" He struck a match to light his pipe, puffing out curling clouds of sickly sweet smoke.

Dada, roused by the increasing passion of both his father's and the president's words, joined in the argument. Between him and Baaba, every pause of the President's speech was soon punctuated with repudiation.

"Yeah, yeah," Dada chided. "Let's see. How about begin by getting control of your cold-blooded military?" My father forced a chip from the stick he was sculpting with his knife.

As if on cue, President Obote launched into discussion of The National Resistance Army, or NRA, a guerilla group headed by Yoweri Museveni. Baaba chewed on his pipe; Dada attacked his stick with renewed vigor.

Museveni and the bulk of his rebel fighters came from the Ankole tribe of western Uganda. Ankole people hold a physical resemblance to the Tutsi, and because of this superficial coincidence, innocent Tutsis had increasingly become targets of the government's anti-rebel violence.

"What about fighting the rebel group and not us because we resemble their leader?" Dada spat.

My sense of belonging, of being one of the "citizens" Obote so passionately called out to, faded altogether, replaced by bitterness and a gnawing feeling of displacement.

"If we are not wanted here, then why can't we go back to Rwanda?" The president's speech had barely ended when the question exploded from me.

Dada looked shocked. "Well," he began. "We tried to return once, but it's not that easy." He paused, squinting his eyes and directing his attention to the static buzz of the poor AM transmission station, as if waiting for the speech to resume.

"Go on, John," Baaba said. "Finish. Explain to Rwabagabo why we can't return to Rwanda. I have done enough explaining to you; it's your turn to talk to your kids about such things."

"Yes," Dada replied. "Give me a minute." He rubbed his palms on his pants, then got up and walked to a nearby hedge. After a thorough study, he removed a branch. Baaba and I remained silent. With a fair bit of throat clearing, Dada settled back into his seat and began sculpting the stick into another *inkoni,* a walking cane. He seemed to have forgotten about my question.

My grandfather took a deep breath, wiped his face with a faded blue handkerchief, and clucked his tongue. "You really do want to know, don't you?" He observed, a smile crinkling his right cheek. "Hmm." He paused. "See, that's a sublime trait, Rwabagabo! That you will sit here patiently and wait for the story of your inheritance. Everyone should know their background, or else they are like the crippling plant without roots that blooms off the mulberry tree. You've got to know your roots!"

Dada clenched his jaw and shot me a curt look. "You and I were born here, so we do not need to go anywhere," he said, and resumed sculpting.

My eyes followed the wood chips falling between Dada's legs. I wondered if we immigrants held a similar destiny: scraped off the main stem and stomped into the ground.

"But if we really wanted to go back?" I asked. "Can't we?"

For a moment, Baaba watched Dada with hard eyes. Finally, he sighed and turned to me. "Do you remember what I told you about the reason we left Rwanda, Rwabagabo?" he asked.

"Yes, yes," I answered. "Something about the foreigners ruining the country's politics—leading to genocide." Fuzzy memories of Baaba's stories swam with the little bits of history I'd learned in school.

A wide grin spread across my grandfather's face. He patted his knees. "You are so good at memorizing things." Clearing his throat and turning to his son, Baaba said, "John, turn the volume down a bit, will you?" Dada complied stiffly.

"In 1944, when I came to Uganda searching for work, the *Bazungu* were still in control of Rwanda." His eyes narrowed as he spat out the Rwandese word for white people.

"I know they were white, but of what origin, Baaba?" At twelve, I knew that white people, though they all looked alike, came from different countries.

"From Belgium. The Tutsis and the Hutus lived in harmony until the *Bazungu* came. The colonists made us carry ethnic identity cards, used propaganda to turn neighbors and families against each other so they could control us and exploit our resources. The Belgians gave a military helicopter to the Hutu army so they could shoot down Tutsis." Baaba suddenly seemed irritated and waved a hand. "But I'm getting ahead of myself. When I first brought my family to Uganda, it was to find work, not to escape violence. My wife became stressed. She didn't enjoy being in a new place and culture with no relatives. I was gone most of the time, she was lonely and overburdened caring for our children all by herself."

Mama called, "Remember to water those cows, Patrick. I know you and your Baaba well; when you start talking, you can go on forever!" She raised an eyebrow and pointed at the jerry cans at her feet, as if to remind me that they would not fill themselves.

"She's right," Dada said standing up. "The cows need water. We better get going." He squinted at the golden horizon as if the sun might slip behind it at any second.

"I will come in a minute," I said to Dada.

Baaba had already begun walking back towards the house and did not reply. "Baaba, please finish telling me the story," I implored.

"You little busy-mind!" said Baaba with a smile. He stroked his temple gently with his index finger. "So, where did I stop?"

"Your wife was upset . . .," I reminded him.

"Aha, yes! She asked that I take her back to Rwanda so she could be near my sister and her relatives. As much as I disliked the thought of us being separated, I liked the idea of her beginning to build us a home in Rwanda, after all, it was my goal to save money to buy land and start my own herd.

"While living with me in Uganda, she bore three children, including your father. He was only two years old when she and the children returned to Rwanda. After escorting them home, I returned to Uganda. I was still working here a few years later, in 1959, when ethnic violence erupted between the Hutus and the Tutsi—the so-called Rwandan Revolution. Tens of thousands of Tutsi were slaughtered by Hutu, with the tools of the *bazungu*. My wife, all our children and many more, fled to avoid being killed simply because of the foreign words printed on a plastic card they carried."

I looked up to see Mama standing on the back porch with a warning finger pointing at me.

"Patrick, come inside and drink a cup of milk so you can go help your father bring in the cattle."

"But Baaba," I said, ignoring her. "I want to understand why the natives in this country don't like us."

"I will continue the story as you drink your milk," he said, pushing himself up from his stool and motioning me to lead the way inside. "During the 1959 genocide, tens of thousands of Rwandan Tutsi fled to Uganda." He shrugged. "We left behind our homes, our land, our families, our wealth. But the poisonous stereotypes the *Bazungu* assigned us we could not leave behind. Rwanda remains a divided nation and, to this day, though many of us would like to go back home, we are not allowed to. We are stuck here." He shrugged again. "Perhaps the Ugandans do not like that anymore than we do."

"That must have been very hard, to move your family so many times." I said, gulping down the creamy milk my mother handed me. It was cool and refreshing from having sat all night and day in the breezy shade of the cook-shack.

"Indeed it was, but guess what? We have achieved a lot since then!" Baaba exclaimed, spreading his hands as if to encompass the lands and homes and herds of cattle owned by our family. He smiled and said, "You must go now. Your father will be upset and you know how that ends."

Nodding consent, I put down my empty mug and walked outside, my grandfather close behind me.

"Rwabagabo," Baaba said, placing a hand on my shoulder. I turned to face him, and he peered at me through a small, wrinkled smile. "This is what you should always remember: we were a tribe subjected to great adversity. But we are also resilient, intrinsically powerful, and blessed with special wisdom!" He gave me a wink. "All right now. I will see you later."

I hurried across the field to catch up to Dada, Baaba's stories echoing in my ears. Energy and hope filled me as I reflected on our journey, our traditions, our troubles, plus Grandpa's courage through it all. *Intrinsically powerful*, he'd called us. I felt the strength running through my body.

Dada and I remained quiet all the way to the well, each lost in our own thoughts. I was so caught up in my musings that it took me a while to realize that it was taking much longer than usual to pull water from the well. I was about to ask Dada what was happening when he explained, "The dry season has arrived early. I think it will be a harsh one."

Inka *(cow)*

The drought became severe; our cows grew thin and produced only a fraction of their usual milk. In early November, a week before I finished my final term at Mr. Reuben's Village School, Dada moved our herd north to graze near the Nile River. The day after school ended, I rode a bike to join him.

Uncle Kafuuko, Dada's youngest brother, had moved Baaba's herd out to the river as well. He escorted me to the family camp. The 30-kilometer trail wound maze-like through uninhabited jungle, scratching our legs as we passed through a vast swath of savannah and then gnarly scrubland thick with thorny grey bushes that ripped at our legs. Uncle Kafuuko's short legs peddled tirelessly as he followed a path that seemed hidden to me until it was under my feet. Knowing that soon I would be traveling this trail on my own to deliver milk to my family, I kept alert for landmarks–a tree overcome with knotty burls here, a mass of vines so thick they appeared to be a shrub there. The prospect of memorizing the entire route was daunting, but soon enough I'd be like my uncle, whistling through the thick jungle, my bike swaying merrily and my gears spinning so fast they would become almost invisible.

As we approached the river, shrubs gave way to bare ground, cracked and worn hard by years of trampling cattle. Layers of impenetrable thickets and shriveled pastures followed; stretching so far it felt like we could be traveling in circles. Finally water-loving green palm trees and papyrus, at first desperate and stunted, began to appear. As we drew closer, the green fronds above us became more vibrant, and the plants taller and thicker until we were alongside the papyrus swamps that I knew bordered the river. Uncle Kafuuko turned to me with a big-toothed smile, his kinky hair bouncing as he rode hands-free, steering around the hummocks and roots with intuitive shifts of his skinny body. "Keep riding and your father will be around that bend," he said, pointing ahead.

As if on cue, Dada emerged from a papyrus thicket thirty feet away. My uncle waved at both of us, and bobbed on down the path towards his camp.

Dada and I lived in a round grass-thatch hut he'd built alongside the papyrus swamp. Before my arrival, he slashed a trail down through the thick grove to reach the river and built a boat-shaped clay trough there for the cattle to drink from. For a half-mile stretch down the river banks, men clustered in similar makeshift huts, clumped together in groups of four or five, each with their own corral to keep cattle when they were not being grazed or watered. The corrals, like the little grass huts, were makeshift structures, little more than sticks stuck in the ground and leaned against each other. The cattle stayed in them, packed tight, groaning in the heat and churning the ground to mud.

As the dry season wore on, the Nile narrowed. We were forced to abandon our private trough and take our herd down to a communal watering spot along an open bank of the river, cleared many years before by fisherman. Dada always tried to avoid this watering spot—and I learned on our first day there that this was not because of the small fee the government charged us to use it.

Sun shone down heavily on the milling groups of cattle and the herdsmen tending to them with shouts and clucks. While waiting our turn to lead our cows down to slake their thirst, we saw a brown heifer break loose from a waiting Tutsi-owned herd to join a native Nyara group at the watering trough. Dada's eyes narrowed and his jaw tightened. "This may not go well," he worried, gaze fixed on the runaway cow as she pushed herself in among the others to pull deeply from the water.

"Just a cow joining theirs?" I asked.

"Exactly, just a cow sharing water," Dada sighed. "But the Nyara despise us Tutsi, and will take any excuse to tell us as much. Just watch. You will be surprised how angry it makes them."

At the bank, a lanky Tutsi herdsman with sun-seared skin tried in vain to chase the heifer back to its herd. He called an apology to the Nyara as he flapped his arms at the stubborn animal.

"Sorry is not enough, but taking your damn cow away will be appreciated," the Nyara replied, striding towards the Tutsi.

The native was dark and stocky, with small bloodshot eyes. The space between his forehead and eyebrows was so narrow that when he frowned, hair from both areas appeared to join. The Tutsi, with his long body, towered over him.

"I am doing my best," he replied in a low, calm tone. His gaze shifted from the errant cow to the approaching Nyara.

"You better hope she carries no infection. Or else I will make you sell off your little herd and return to Rwanda. Do you hear me, long nose?"

The final question was gratuitous; his threats were loud enough that even Dada and I heard them clearly.

Seeing an opportunity to get between his cow and the trough, the Tutsi ignored the approaching Nyara and managed to chase the cow back towards her herd. His success was short-lived. The thirsty animal would have none of it; she wanted to finish drinking. Once again, she escaped.

"I see you have failed. I will come and show you how to treat such cows." The Nyara jumped out of the water, grabbed a discarded bamboo branch that lay by the

111

trough, and swung. The thud of the wood against the animal's ribs resounded in the air and sent her reeling back from the trough. She screamed in pain.

Beside me, Dada shifted his *inkoni* into both hands. "That is not good," he muttered darkly. "You do not hit someone's *inka* like that, not a Tutsi–owned cow!"

My eyes fixed on the heifer as she swung her head and hobbled in confused circles, bellowing in low tones. Then I saw her owner striding towards the grinning Nyara. He dropped his stick and rushed the smaller man, tackling him in a clay trench. Muddy water splashed as the Nyara struggled to escape from the Tutsi's strong grip.

"Look what he is doing, Dada!" I cried. The idea of witnessing a drowning sent a cold shudder up my spine despite the searing sun.

Finally, the Tutsi man released the Nyara. As his opponent sputtered to the surface, the Tutsi walked back and retrieved his *inkoni.* Polished and heat-hardened, the stickhad the shape and size of a police baton. I recognized the fighting grip he used to hold it from Baaba's instructions long ago. He paced half circles around the trench like a lion stalking its prey.

As the Nyara shook himself off, two teenage boys gripping heavy stones rushed in from the amassing crowd to join him. One handed him a long machete, its sharp blade catching the light reflected from the river. They began to advance on the lone Tutsi.

"What are we going to do?" I asked Dada. My stomach felt sick.

"Stay here, son. Watch the cows," he replied. He waved me back and rushed to the side of the Tutsi.

"Come back, Dada!" I yelled.

He made no reply, only a hand signal telling me to stay put and watch the herd.

I chewed my lip in dread. The trip home would be a voyage from hell if I had to take my father back wounded or dead. What could I do?

From all sides, herdsmen's eyes left their thirsty, agitated cattle to focus on the fight. Insults and menacing gestures filled the air between the opposing men. The tension and sound of increasingly unmanaged cattle created a wall around them. I could bear it no longer. I threw a last look at my restless herd, then ran to join Dada. A Nyara man approached from the other side of the trough, his stride mirroring mine. As I fell in at Dada's side, I looked back to see our cows moving towards the same well where the conflict started. There was nothing to be done about it now.

"You dimwitted Tutsis disgust me," the old Nyara man screamed. "Why couldn't you keep your stupid cow away? Now, you will return to Rwanda bleeding or dead." The insults the older men uttered made those of Muwonge and the other bullies at school seem mild and weak. With each searing word, the previous pain tore wide again. Now it went even deeper, and a new kind of soreness opened in my soul. How could grown men still speak to each other in such a way?

But it wasn't just the natives throwing insults. Soon, venomous words began to spill form my father's mouth as well. "You dogs!" he shouted, the veins in his neck bulging, eyes dark with rage. "You get any closer and I will smash you to pieces." He pounded his right fist into the palm of his left hand. "Damn fools who know nothing beyond their village!" he spat. Then he threw a hard glance at me, standing by his shoulder. Clearly, he had mixed feelings about my presence there.

The threats flew as we circled in on each other until we were so close I could see the spittle flying from angry lips. Dada kept his eyes on his opponents, but seemed to sense where I was beside him. Every time I tried to advance, his arm flew up to push me back.

Here we were, men reduced to primitive beasts, circling each other with hard fists and narrow minds.

Baaba said we Tutsis were a people with intrinsic power and great wisdom! Wasn't this a wise time to exercise that intrinsic power—in a conflict where we were so obviously outnumbered? Did we have a choice?

A tense silence quivered through the group as the threats gave way to snarls. Behind us the gathering crowd watched. The acrid smell of fear mixed with cow dung and decaying vegetation filled the air. Muscles tensed. My mind stilled, preparing to fight. Then, a voice from the forest snapped: "People, people, help!" It was a little boy's shrill call. "The bulls are fighting, their horns are locked! Help, help!" he pleaded.

The impatient herds, left untended as the men crowded in to fight or watch, chose that moment to stampede towards the drinking trough.

Chaos broke the fight. Men raced every which way, trying to protect the clay drinking troughs from being crushed by the mass of uncontrolled cattle, no longer mindful of whose herd belonged to whom. In the midst of it all, the fighting bulls filled the air with frantic bellows that rose above the thud of hooves.

"You may have survived a beating today, but it isn'tover," the older Nyara man yelled. "We will find you and all of you will pay! You'll pay big, you worthless foreigners!"He spun off to recover his herd, the teenagers at his heels.

"We are used to those threats. Come fight or go to hell!" the Tutsi man hollered back.

"Cowards!" Dada mumbled. "That fool is right, though, Kabanda," he said to the Tutsi man, who walked beside us. "It isn't over, but you know what? It has never been over for our Tutsi race; they find ways to hurt us. We are like the Jews, still fighting to be recognized in their own land."

Kabanda shook his head in frustrated agreement, his lips still quivering from the fight.

Ahead of us, a group of men yelled and threatened the fighting bulls with sticks. Distracted by the stampede, the bulls disengaged with final snorts and trotted off to join their herds.

Clucks and shouts filled the air. Gradually the men managed to separate their herds. The cows were lathered and sweaty, their eyes rolling in fear and excitement. "This is a mess," Dada said, swatting a cow forward. The community troughs were now little more than a series of mud pits. "It's going to cost some money and labor to rebuild."

The icy drip of neglected responsibility ran down my spine. "I know you wanted me to manage the herd, but I couldn't stand back while you fought," I told Dada, unsure of what I wanted his response to be.

"Young man," Kabanda interjected with an indulgent smile. "This is in no way your fault." He gestured with his stick to encompass the hundreds of cattle being prodded back into their respective groups. "You could not have controlled five thirsty herds—not alone."

By evening the cows, contained and calm, returned to the Nile camps. Kabanda and my father stood around a crackling fire at our camp, drinking *waragi* and musing over the day's events. I wanted to stay and listen to the men talk, but it was my responsibility to deliver milk home to the family. I piled the jerry cans on the back of my bike and raced against the unfolding darkness, accentuated by the jungle with its consuming shadows. The trail consumed my focus entirely; I couldn't allow my mind a second to wander back to the fight.

*   *   *

Baaba was at home waiting for me. Of course, he already knew of the fight and my Dada's involvement in it. Someone in the village could get engaged or accepted into university, and it seemed that my grandfather would know about it before anyone else.

As I heaved the jerry can off the bicycle carrier, I prepared for an earful.

"Rwabagabo! I am glad to see you safe and still standing tall." In the grey light I could see a small but proud smile on his face.

"I was really scared, Baaba."

"Those are wicked men," he replied. "Anybody would be afraid of them. However, we cannot cower and let wickedness prevail by intimidation. I'm glad you stood up for your tribe and your family, and for what is right. I mean, who hits a cow for sharing cow water?" He sighed and took his eyes away from me for a moment while his gaze wandered off.

I pulled a bench up to the veranda and sat down next to my grandfather. Fatigue crept through my body and mind for the first time that day. I struggled to fight its heavy wash, wanting to hear more of Baaba's opinions.

Especially now, my mind empty with exertion, it seemed

better to hear his ideas than work on forming my own.

"Cows are animals! Innocent animals!" Baaba

continued. "No excuse to hit them for following instinct."

He patted me on the shoulder, causing my elbow to slide

off my thigh. I caught myself like someone aroused from a

nap.

"You must be tired, little man," Baaba said, his

voice becoming gentle. "You should ask your mother for

food and get some sleep."

"No, I just rode my bicycle too fast," I said,

straightening and trying to widen my eyes. "I delayed

leaving because of the conflict. I hate the darkness of the

jungle on that route, Baaba!"

"I am proud of you, your father, and Kabanda for

standing up to those bullies," Baaba spat out the last words.

He waved his hand as if he didn't care that he had insulted

them.

"If it wasn't for the bulls, and the destruction of the water trough, it would have been a lot worse," I replied. "It was very dangerous, Baaba."

"I know! And of course it was not only about a cow drinking from their trough; that is just another excuse. They do not like us and they do not want us here. We face this when we try to get medical care, or buy food at the market, or travel the roadways—in everything!" He thumped his large fist on the wooden bench we shared.

"What have we Tutsi done to earn this curse, to pass it in our blood to our children so they must carry it too?"Baaba lamented. A cool evening breeze rustled the trees around us, and he shifted to fling his *Igitengi*—a square, colorful cotton jacket—over his back. He sighed. "Besides hating us, many natives underestimate us."

From my grandfather's house, Auntie Kamugudu called, "Baaba, you need to come eat dinner; it's getting cold."

"Rwabagabo, don't worry," Baaba consoled as he rose to leave. "Today we are still pursued—from all sides it seems—by devilish racists and bigots, but things will work out. They will be better for your generation. You keep excelling at school—keep showing them the cleverness and intelligence of the Tutsi in the classroom. The more battles we can win with our minds, the less we will have to fight with our fists."

Baaba left me with a smile and walked towards his house. Night engulfed him as if a dark curtain had closed behind him.

*   *   *

I stayed outside for another moment, thinking about my grandfather's words. As always, they stirred me, and I took them as truth. We Tutsi bore a curse. When and how would it end? I would choose to fight for respect using my mind—my inherent Tutsi wisdom—but I would not be afraid to use my fists again if necessary. Things would get better for my generation. I would help make them better. What I didn't know then, though I wonder sometimes if my intuitive old Baaba did, was that they would get far worse first.

Five

March 1983 *(Baale, Uganda)*

Mweso *(Board game)*

When the drought ended, Kabanda, the proud Rwandese who fought the Nyara at the Nile, rode up on his bicycle. I was outside, stapling barbed wire onto the posts to seal off a break in the cattle fence. The formalities of his dress—a cowboy hat, checkered shirt tucked under a pair of cotton pants, and leather shoes—alerted me that this was not a casual visit. As I walked forward to greet him, he leaned his bicycle against the kraal, giving the aging posts a slight push to assure they would hold its weight. Beads of sweat dripped down his face and neck, and he pulled out a white handkerchief to wipe them as he greeted me.

His voice and eyes expressed a warm sense of solidarity, causing me to recall with pride what it had felt like to fight beside him. I felt tall and proud as I turned away to fetch my father.

"One more thing, young man," Kabanda called. I paused, and he continued. "My wife told me about your amazing reading skills. How are your studies going? I know that school begins again soon."

Unable to hide my happiness at the compliment, I smiled broadly and replied, "I have been reading whenever I get time."

"I think your father should find you a better school," he suggested.

"I don't know if Dada—" Before I could relay my father's apparent disinterest in my education, my mother appeared in the doorway.

"Look who's here!" She cried. Her big dark eyes sparkled. "We are so glad to see you."

"Thank you," said Kabanda. "You have an intelligent chap here. We were just talking about his school."

"Is that right? You can say he's intelligent for chasing butterflies, or playing with that lazy dog all day," she joked.

They continued with good-natured small talk as I headed off to fetch Dada. Following the heavy thump of his axe, I found him over the hillside, felling a camphor tree.

"Kabanda is here to see you," I called out.

"Oh, okay," he replied, his words coming in between rhythmic swings. "I will be right up."

Back at the house, my father greeted Kabanda while I went inside to retrieve a wooden chair and a clean shirt for Dada. When I returned, Kabanda's wide grin and lively gestures had been replaced by a chilling sobriety. Dada, his eyes fixed on his friend, did not even look my way as he took the shirt from my hands and pulled the chair beneath him to sit.

"I am here to discuss some issues, John," Kabanda said, leaning forward on his stool and clasping his hands respectfully. He took a deep breath and his eyes softened a bit. "First, I'm inviting you to my daughter's wedding. Will you come?"

"Yes, of course, my friend. But why the somber face when speaking of such a joyous occasion?"

"Well, it's nothing new; but that is the other reason I am here," Kabanda said.

I noticed my father stiffen, and felt suddenly awkward where I stood beside his chair. Kabanda might think of me as a man, but my father still looked at me as a twelve-year-boy. He refused to have me around when discussing important issues. Before he could turn around and embarrass me with a dismissal, I bobbed my head to Kabanda and disappeared out the door.

Of course, I still wanted to know what they would

say—and I knew I wouldn't be able to get it out of Dada later. The old mulberry tree next to the house made a great place to eavesdrop. I tiptoed over to its trunk to catch the conversation taking place behind our home's thin mud walls, my ears tuning out the hoots of my siblings playing inside the house.

"By the way," Kabanda was saying. "Thanks for standing by me at the Nile."

"Of course!" Dada exclaimed. "They ganged up on me earlier this year when I tried to reclaim a cow. Everyone, including their relatives, knew they had stolen it. Those narrow-minded Nyaras will find any excuse to use their machetes against one of our kind." His words ended with a derisive Tutsi "tisk tisk."

"John Kafuniza," Kabanda said to my father, his voice growing so low that I had to slide close and press my ear to the wall to hear it. "I am afraid that soon they will need no excuse to use those machetes against us. President

Obote is planning to remove all Rwandese from Uganda and send them back to Rwanda. Idi Amin did it with the Indians," he added, referring to the former ruler's violent ninety-day expulsion of virtually all of the country's Indians and Asians in 1972. "Now it will be done to us."

"The other day, the local chief came and warned me. I was impressed and grateful that he would risk himself to do so," I heard Dada say.

From the back of the house I heard Mama call to them, "Would you men like some chai or water?"

A brief moment passed, neither one said anything. The air felt heavy and toxic around me, the anxiety of the impending suffering brought me to my feet.

"That is very kind of you, Mrs. Kafuniza," I heard Kabanda reply. "But I was just leaving."

"Patrick," Mama called out, "Come and say goodbye to Mr. Kabanda."

I stepped lightly away from my hiding spot and

took a deep breath before plastering what I hoped was a look of serene innocence on my face. I walked around the corner of the house. From the looks on Kabanda and Dada's faces, they did not suspect me. "Farewell to you, Mr. Kabanda," I said. His face was drawn when I met his eyes, and my words brought only a shallow smile.

"Be well, young man," he replied. "Don't forget to read your books."

*   *   *

The following afternoon, Baaba and I sat in his yard playing *Mweso*, a game similar to checkers. Players move coffee beans between 32 pits carved into a wooden board, and though the play can be rapid and consuming, it's also an easy game. I relaxed into the cool air and orange sky of the East African sunset and intentionally let Baaba win game after game, hoping he'd realize I had something else on my mind. This strategy always worked.

Mid-play through our fourth game he paused while reaching to move a set of beans, cleared his throat, and placed his hand on his knees. "So, Rwabagabo, what's the matter?" he asked. Instead of taking his turn, he began returning the beans carefully to their holes. Once he was done, he stretched his aging back and let his deep, red-rimmed eyes settle on me.

"Two days ago, the administrator came to our house, and last night Mr. Kabanda came," I said, meeting his gaze as firmly as I could. "All these meetings: what's going on?"

Baaba's hand rose. "What do you mean?"

"I overheard Dada tell Mama about being gone for some time, but I don't understand why. You know he never tells me much." I pushed the *Mweso* game aside.

A curl in Baaba's upper lip appeared. He used his raised palm to wipe his mouth from one corner to the other.

"It isn't anything we can't handle, young man. Remember, we are the Tutsis!"

"Baaba, I know something is wrong," I persisted.

"It is not for your age," he replied, eyeing me sadly. But I read contemplation on his face, and knew I could push on.

"I'm almost twelve! And I heard Dada tell Kabanda something about sending us out of the country. If this is true, you must tell me why."

Baaba sighed and brought his sweaty hands to rest upon his thighs. When he spoke his words were slow and clear. "All right, Rwabagabo, all right. It seems you have heard enough that it is my duty to tell you more." He cleared his throat. "The current government is telling all people to register to vote in the upcoming elections. At the registration, all Ugandans will be issued national identity cards--all except for those who are Tutsi. This way, they will be able to isolate and expel us." He sighed, and a sad smile pulled on one corner of his mouth. "It is much like what happened to us in Rwanda. The curse of the Tutsi."

As if the space between us could steal Baaba's words from me, I leaned in closer and asked, "What about Tutsis who were born in Uganda?"

"The government is denying all of us the cards. What you have to understand is that this all is happening now because of a guerilla fighter seen as a threat by the regime."

"A guerilla fighter?" I wracked my memory for the name I'd heard during the independence speeches months ago. "Do you mean Yoweri Museveni?"

"You have keen ears. Yes. And Museveni is not alone. He has many people supporting him. They call themselves the National Resistance Army." Baaba shrugged. "Perhaps Obote is right to be afraid."

"But he is Ugandan, isn't he? What does he have to do with the Tutsi?"

"This is where it becomes complicated," he explained. "Museveni comes from the Ankole tribe in western Uganda. That tribe is allowed to obtain national I..D but not us, the Tutsis of Rwanda. The government has a task army—the Special Forces—whose job is to find and kill anyone who may be assisting the rebel cause. They are not very selective. As you know most Ugandans do not want us here. Because of our resemblance to the rebel leader's tribe, every Tutsi is a target, regardless of their involvement with the NRA."

"But . . . do we have involvement with this rebel group?"

Baaba sat up a little straighter. "Oh yes, the NRA is full of our people." He cast a quick glance around and then moved closer, capped his big hands onto my ear, and whispered, "We have a few relatives fighting in Museveni's army."

"We do?" I asked, sitting back with a start, my

voice coming out louder than I intended.

Baaba winked, and raised a finger to his lips to imply secrecy.

Calling out from the front door of our house, mama cut off our conversation with a loud reminder that I was late fetching water.

Baaba half-closed his eyes and nodded. Though he seemed sorry to end our talk, he waved me off with a leathery hand. I was beginning to learn that the more answers I found, the more questions followed. I slung the metal water cans over my shoulders and set off for the well, thoughts spinning in my head.

Would the government really try to force us out of our country? And poor Baaba! Chased out of his home long ago, he came here looking for peace. Now, in old age and with his strength long gone, he was facing the same threat again. The curse of the Tutsi. Would we never have a place we could call home?

I recalled Baaba's words when I came back from the fight at the Nile: that we must not let wickedness prevail because we are being intimidated or threatened. This was our land—we were born here. We could not be forced to leave simply because of the color of our skin or the lankiness of our limbs. Why should we run away before their threats? Baaba himself said that Museveni had a large following— that the government should be scared of his NRA. Perhaps our relatives were right to stand up and fight.

The sun burned the horizon and cast languid shadows across the savannah. Soon it would disappear, pulling with it the naiveté of my youth. Who knew what would be born out of the darkness that followed.

Agatare *(Communal Market)*

The next day was market day in Baale town. After tending

to the cattle, Dada and I set out by bicycle to cover the five-kilometer dirt road leading to the trading center. I sat on the front carrier, reaching behind to hold onto the handlebars as we bumped and hopped over potholes in the road. At first, Dad pedaled in silence. The trees blurred by, and my mind wandered off.

"Patrick, soon I will be making a trip south, to the Rwandan border."

"To the border, Dada?" I asked, confused. His words caught me off guard. They seemed unconnected to reality. Why would Dada be traveling to the border?

He cleared his throat and I felt the bike surge as his feet spun faster. "Baaba tells me he has explained to you some of the dangers we Tutsi face right now, especially in Uganda's current political situation. Our family may need to leave the country. I must be familiar with the route we would take."

I did not reply, but gripped the bike tighter. My

mind felt as if it had been drenched by a bucket of freezing water.

"These are complicated, adult matters," he said. "But you have come of age. I wouldn't want us to be in a situation you weren't aware of."

I barely registered the importance of those words, of my father declaring my manhood. The reality of leaving our home overwhelmed me.

"Leave Uganda? Why can't we stay and fight?" I asked, my heart thumping.

Dada didn't answer. Silence stretched on for minutes. When he finally spoke, it was not to answer my question. Instead, he said, "Patrick, I understand you are scared. It is okay for a man to be scared, but it is his responsibility to take charge regardless. Controlling fear is what makes some men brave. Losing control is a risk in itself."

Dada had never talked to me that way. And now . . .

he had told me I was a man, and said he would be leaving the family in my care while he embarked on a dangerous mission. The implications of the conversation whispered at the corners of my mind, but I felt too overwhelmed to confront them. Drooping trees and thorny bushes bobbed in the steaming heat. I felt as though I was seasick with their saturated colors. My father sensed my discomfort. "Would you like to peddle the rest of the distance?" he offered.

We switched places, and as my legs worked and my breath came harder, my thoughts grew smooth and organized. Despite the exertion of pedaling the bike, my pulse evened out; I no longer felt that my heart would thud its way out of my chest. The old gears of the bicycle hummed with the rhythm of my pistoning legs.

"I need to buy pants for my trip," Dada said from where he sat on the bicycle carrier. "The kind with hidden pockets for concealing money."

"Hide money? Why?" I asked.

He chuckled. "The Special Forces will dig into your ass if they think they can find money there."

"Wow! They must be crazy," I joined in on the laughter, ignorant of the cold truth behind Dada's words.

"If you bear any physical resemblance to the rebel fighters, they will take anything of value that they find on you," he continued in serious voice. "If you're lucky, that is all they will do."

He cleared his throat and added in a low and tight voice, "They have no problem with killing a Tutsi."

The unfamiliar cold undertone in his voice drew in silence with it. The thought of his death was heavy between us. In my head, questions again tumbled upon each other, and I struggled to choose which ones to voice. Dada had no problem shutting down interrogation with silence, but if I was careful with my words I might be able to find the answers I desperately needed.

"How many check-points are there, Dada?"

"Countless! Every town has a check-point these days. I will be clear and honest with you, Patrick. This is not a safe journey. Since this began, I know of one friend tortured and another killed. Neither of them were part of the guerilla group." He shook his head in frustration. "But that is why so many Tutsis have joined the rebels." "We are treated like them regardless. The government gives us no choice."

Silence fell between us, but soon was lost to the din of Baale town. The daunting reality of my father's mortality and the possibility of having to leave the only home I'd ever known overwhelmed me. I barely noticed that we'd entered the town center until a young man carrying a huge burlap sack of corn almost collided with our bicycle. The shouts and clatters of the marketplace rose as those of my perturbed mind. The aroma of fried cassava and ripe bananas flooded my nostrils.

Throngs of traders and buyers milled before crumbling brick-walled shops with sheet-iron roofs stained orange with rust. Set back from the sidewalk, a woman squatted to ladle tea from a steaming cook-pot set over a small fire, while a man repaired bicycles under a mango tree. A truck lurched feebly along, and an occasional motorcycle pushed past the bicycles and pedestrians on the gravel streets.

Five men racing on their bicycles swerved around us. Seconds later, a little girl dashed out from behind a potato farmer hawking his wares. Suddenly, the racing bikers were upon her, her body thrown beneath their tires.

I hit the brakes, but Dada had already jumped down from his seat on the handlebars. He hit the ground running towards the fallen girl. The offenders hadn't even slowed and were nowhere to be seen.

On Dada's command, I moved our bike to attempt to block oncoming traffic from trampling the crying child.

Blood matted her short, kinky hair and streamed down her forehead and into her eyes. The side of one leg was a dark mess of ripped skin and embedded gravel, her dress torn and dirty.

After checking gently to make sure it was safe to move her, Dada scooped her up and carried her off the road. Hearing her wails, a woman appeared from a kiosk nearby. Tears welled in her large, dark eyes and began to track brown rivers in the town-dust on her cheeks as she took the slight frame gently into her arms.

"She is going to be okay," Dada reassured me as we watched the crowd swallow them. He wiped gravel and blood from his hands, not seeming to notice the rough black streaks he left on the thighs of his pants. "Just when you think war is the only risk," he spat, "man finds another way to hurt his own kind!"

"She is so young and innocent," I said quietly. "I wonder why God didn't protect her."

Up ahead, I could hear the marketplace, the squawks of chickens kept in stick cages, the shouts of traders haggling. The street widened to a broad plaza, where traders sat under tents, umbrellas, and tree canopies with their wares spread out before them on colorful grass mats. In one of the stalls, a vendor surely had a pair of pants with a hidden pocket. Without that pocket, my father wouldn't be able to journey to the border to map our escape route. Is that all God had to give us for protection? A pocket?

Dada sensed my frustration. "That is not how God operates, son," he replied. "*He* is too big for our little minds to comprehend. If we understood him we would be gods ourselves." Above us a flock of birds cawed and swooped before alighting in a graceful cloud atop a rusting roof. My father watched them and said, "We cannot ask God to justify himself to us. We can only pray for his guidance, and for the strength to follow it."

Six

February, 1984 (Baale, Uganda)

Balaro *(Cattle keepers)*

Classes resumed, and my newly acquired adult stresses
eased to the back of my mind, replaced temporarily with
those of attending fifth grade in a new school.

On a breezy Monday morning, Joyce, Robinah and I
headed off together for our first day at Baale Primary.
Unlike the dark jungle trail to Mr. Reuben's school, the
more-trafficked road to town spread wide and wound
through open land. I still found myself sorely missing the
comforting mother-hen protection of Rosette. With barely a
week's notice, my parents had sent her away to live with

our grandmother in the Buruli district of Uganda.

"It was time for her to find a husband," my father explained, "Her chances of marrying into a good home are better in that region." His explanation did nothing to soothe me—I felt as though our already threatened family was being unnecessarily torn apart.

Despite missing Rosette and despite the grumbling in our stomachs and the harsh gravel beneath our feet, my sisters and I were soon in good spirits as the two-and-a-half hour walk to school wound on. Sunrise played coloring games with the horizon, changing the rolling savannah around us from orange to golden to screaming yellow. Song birds swooped and chirped from clumps of trees. We talked about what our new teachers would be like. I happily jingled the money mother had slipped into my pocket to buy pancakes for lunch.

*   *   *

"Here we are!" Joyce gasped happily when Baale town came into view.

Our pace quickened. Ahead, a group of uniformed children came into view. They seemed to be standing in line outside a compound of small, rusty-roofed buildings. "Is that the school?" Robinah queried, pointing at the group.

"Yes!" I exclaimed. "Can we run now? I'm afraid we are late already."

Without waiting for a reply, I started to jog. My sisters followed. We were all well aware of the consequences of being late to Mr. Reuben's school.

Even the stirring of those unpleasant memories couldn't quell our good cheer. With a smirk, Robinah pushed ahead of me. I responded by picking up my feet a little faster. Soon all three of us were in full out sprint, racing barefoot towards the school yard. We tumbled to a stop at the back of the group. Our gasping laughter cut short as a scream ripped the air.

Looking about I noticed the painful drawn faces on the kids we'd joined. Around the corner, a little girl gathered her books from the ground, tears running down her face, shoulders shaking.

Past her, a boy was pinned beneath the foot of a heaving woman—presumably a teacher. She raised a thin, flexing cane and brought it whipping down on his bottom. His scream ripped the air again, bringing a rabid grimace to the heavy woman's loose face. Her little reptilian eyes, sunken into dark folds, squinted with manic rage. A knee-high, yellow dress clung tightly over her bulging abdomen.

I grabbed my sisters and backed slowly away.

Panic rattled my legs as we joined the line. There did not seem any other way to enter the school.

Like a rhinocerosgoring a deer out of its way, the teacher pushed the next little girl in line and forced her onto the ground. She raised the cane, hesitated for a moment, and then hit the child hard, issuing a muffled screech—I could see the little girl biting down her own arm to keep from crying out.

I studied the current victim, wondering if she might be Tutsi, though from her square face and narrow forehead, she appeared to be Nyara. I guessed the teacher was of the same tribe. At least she did not seem to discriminate in her administration of punishment. As I studied the hulking beast in the yellow dress, her little eyes rose from the girl's backside to meet mine.

"Who are these slender ones?" she rumbled, breasts still heaving from exertion of the many lashings she'd already administered. "I can tell you are *Balaro*," she said, calling us cattle keepers, a condescending term used by native Ugandans.

The little Nyara girl pushed herself up and scurried out of reach, hiding her wet face behind her books.

The teacher tapped the side of her leg with a cane and looked at us inquisitively. Her gaze shifted from me to Robinah and then to Joyce.

None of us spoke. Joyce took a little step backwards, stumbling as she bumped into my stiff body. Robinah, face pale and eyes unfocused, seemed about to faint. I put an arm out to steady her.

"Are you new to this school?" the teacher addressed Joyce.

"Yes, Madame," my sister replied in a weak voice.

The teacher laughed in an ugly ripping sound. "You are so scared, you can't even breathe!" She raised her cane and Joyce flinched again, instinctively bringing her hands to shield her face. "This is what will happen to you if you come to school late," she growled. "Since this is your first day and you do not know what time we begin, punishment will not be administered."

She dropped the cane to her side and fixed her

beady gaze on us.

Unsure of what to do next, I began to lead my sisters forward towards the buildings.

"Stop, you idiots!" The teacher roared, hoisting the cane again. "In this school, you can't go anywhere without my permission first!"

We froze stock still, squeezed together like three newly-weaned calves, trembling with fright. The silence stretched on, so I began to request permission.

But just as the words were about to leave my mouth, she snapped. "Do you see the middle building?" Her cane whipped through the air towards a small hut twenty meters away.

"Yes," we replied in quaking unison.

"That is the headmaster's office. He will register you and send you to your respective classes." My legs wavered when I tried to move, but I still wasn't sure we'd been granted permission. Again the silence stretched on a moment too long, and the request once again trembled at the brink of my lips when she yelled, "Go there now!"

Before she'd finished, Robinah broke out in a run, leading the three of us in a panicked dash to the presumed safety of the office building. At least we'd be away from the rabid anger of the teacher. As we passed the middle quadrangle, a group of class captains, identified by a special badge on their shirt, kicked dirt in our direction and snarled with laughter.

The rest of the day none of us stepped out of our classrooms except to meet the demands of our bladders. As soon as school ended, we fled for home.

Imbunda *(Gun)*

That evening I ate dinner restlessly, then buried myself in my studies. I missed the thrill of learning, the places and questions books opened in my head. It was a relief to escape back into those written worlds, especially with all of the stress building in my real one.

It was late, the candles burning low, when old Nyabwangu, out of character began barking wildly. As I tried to shush him, a heavy knock sounded at the door. Nyabwangu's fervor increased. Dada got up from his chair in the corner and went to answer the door, waving his hand at the old dog which whined and settled into a restrained, whimpering growl.

From where I sat near the door, I could just hear the words from behind it. Though my younger siblings continued about their play and activities, Mama's hand paused on her weaving as she too listened intently.

"Who's there?" Dada asked.

"It's me, Gabo," a husky voice answered, low as a whisper.

"Gabo?" Dada asked, pressing his ear to the door.

"Gabo: your maternal cousin. Open for me, John

Kafuniza," the voice said, a little louder this time.

Dada cautiously unbolted the door, opened it halfway, and said, "Cousin! Good to see you! It's been a long time. Come in!"

"Wait, John," Gabo said. "I need to talk to you first. Can you come out for a second?" In the doorway, I could make out a tall, silhouetted figure.

As Dada stepped outside, Mama and I moved silently towards the door. Dada had left it open a crack, and we pressed close to make out the low voices.

"Cousin," we heard my father ask, "Why are you carrying *Imbunda*? You are scaring me with those guns."

Mama's hand gripped my shoulder; I could feel her trembling. We pressed closer to the door, and I felt my bladder weaken but a moment later my muscles tensed for confrontation.

"I'm sorry, cousin." Gabo replied, his voice a little softer. "I didn't mean to. Please relax, you are safe with us."

"Are you serious? How can I relax?"

"Step away from the door, John," Gabo replied, irritation creeping into his voice. "And keep your voice down; your kids will hear us."

"No. Gabo, if you are going to take me---just shoot me--but spare my family, please," Dada said, his voice trembling.

I reached out to open the door but Mama slapped my hand down with a sharp deterring stare.

"Shoot you? I could never do that. You're family." Gabo cleared his throat, and his rasping voice became soothing once again. "In fact, the reason I am here is that our government is planning to kill us all."

"That much I know," Dada replied nervously. "So do the rest of the Tutsis."

"Correct, cousin. So you know we cannot sit chewing our cud while they slay us like so many cows in a *kraal*. Please come closer, I will explain."

There was a shuffling of feet, and two or three more indistinguishable voices as the men moved out of earshot.

"Do you think Gabo is working for the Special Forces?" I asked Mama in a low whisper.

"I don't know. If he is, then they have used him to come and take your father away." Tears quivered at the corners of her eyes. "Your father would not be the first man in this village to become a victim."

"I swear I will join the rebel group and fight back," I barked.

"Shush, don't talk like that, Patrick." She wiped away tears and gave me another stern look. "God will prevail."

Behind us, my siblings grew uneasy. They paced and quarreled, repeatedly edging closer to us and then scurrying off when mama shushed them and waved them away.

Curiosity gnawed at me like a rabid woodchuck, as I trembled with the urge to burst through the door and stand beside my father. It seemed like hours passed before he finally returned.

"Florence," Dada scolded as he slipped through the door. "Keep the children inside--and quiet!" He cleared his throat. "We have some special guests tonight." My siblings quieted and turned their faces up to listen. "There are four men, coming from Luwero district—many days travel to the East. One of them is my cousin. He used to live with us when all of you were just babies."

"John," Mama said, laying her long, slender hand on his forearm. "Who are the men with Gabo?" Her fingers clamped tight, as if by holding onto him she could stop the words that tumbled from her mouth. It didn't work. "What's going on, John? Are we safe?"

"They are all Gabo's men. They have guns and lots of ammunition. But don't be alarmed." False confidence deepened his voice but did little to counteract the effect of his words.

"How can I not be alarmed?" Mama said tersely. "Armed men, in the middle of the night?"

"Florence, calm yourself." Dada shifted his gaze towards me and my sisters.

The children stood wide-eyed and silent. I wondered what they understood.

"They are on a mission," my father explained.

My mother instinctively reached down and pulled her youngest two towards her. They clung to her legs, tears beginning to streak their cheeks. "And they will bring these weapons into our house?" She shook her head in protest.

"Look here, Florence," my father spat, irritation pushing through his veneer of calm. "They are fighters, for goodness sake. What do you expect, for them to walk around with sticks?"

My mother blinked at him. All of her daughters

were now at her legs, huddled close, gazing up at our father. I stood a little off to the side, listening intently to the conversation. "I will say one last thing, husband. It is something you already know." Her long arms wrapped protectively around the children and she met him with an unwavering gaze. "If the government's forces learn of this, we will all be slaughtered like pigs in a pen."

"These people are fighting for our freedom," Dada replied, meeting the intensity of her gaze. "If we do not support them, and they fail, then we will have to give up everything we have ever owned and flee the country to start all over again." He hesitated a moment before adding, "If we are not 'slaughtered like pigs' as we flee."

My mother's firm voice began to crack as she replied, "I don't know what to think, John. You are putting us in a terrible situation."

"We don't have a choice, Florence," Dada insisted. "We can't escape the risk of death. Either we face it running, or we face it fighting."

My mother's shoulders softened, her proud chin dropping to her chest in resignation. She nodded.

"Go," Dada said, touching her arm tenderly. "Tend to the children. I will speak to the men."

*   *   *

Dada returned shortly, followed closely by four young men with faces hidden under battered baseball caps. I'd never met my uncle, Gabo, but I recognized the family resemblance as he smiled and ducked through our low doorway. His long nose and coffee-colored skin suggested Tutsi heritage, while lanky arms cradled a semi-automatic rifle. The other three men were shorter and darker. They carried their AK-47s close to their chests. For a minute there was only the clomp of heavy-soled combat boots and a shuffling of gear as they clicked off black metal flashlights and piled their faded canvas backpacksin a corner. The rank odor of cigarettes and stale sweat filled the room.

While Gabo greeted me and my siblings with a big smile and friendly words, the other men slid down along the walls of the house, drew their knees to their chests, and sat wordlessly. They kept their heads down low, faces shielded by the brims of their hats, not wanting us to recognize their faces.

Mama disappeared, then came back bearing cups of milk and plates of posho and fried beans. My sisters moved about shyly in the shadows while the men wolfed down their food like jackals tearing a carcass. Milk dripped thin streaks through the scruff of their jaws; beans stuck to their dirt-stained fingers.

"How is my Auntie?" Gabo asked before cramming more beans into his already full mouth.

"Mom is fine," Dada answered. "She will be shocked to know you were here."

A look of sadness flashed over Gabo's face. He swallowed and wiped his lips with the back of his hand. "It's been ten years since I last saw her." He shook his head and glanced in the direction of grandma's house, as if he could catch a glimpse of her through the walls and the darkness. "I hope I will have a chance to visit soon. Our commanders give us strict orders regarding where to go. If I disobey, I could endanger many lives—including my own."

"I understand," Dada replied.

"Please extend my greetings and tell her I'm sorry."

"No need to apologize," Dada said. "She will be sorry to have missed you, but she will understand."

Gabo forced a smile and sighed deeply.

"Cousin John," he said, spreading his arms wide. "You have a beautiful family. And thank you for housing us."

"It's the least I can do. Right now I have my family

to care for, so . . ." he left the thought with a conspiratorial nod that Gabo returned. Mama, engaged in fixing a mistake in the basket my sister Annet was weaving, missed the implications of the exchange, but I did not. *So I cannot fight beside you.*

The rest of their conversation blurred as I pictured my father, huddled with Gabo and these men, a rifle slung over his back, tactics flying in hushed voices. In my mind, I grabbed a gun and stepped in beside them. They welcomed me with gruff nods, and widened their circle so I could join.

When I looked up, the men had licked their plates clean and pushed them to the side. "You must be as tired as dogs," Dada was saying. "Lord knows how I would feel after a fifty-kilometer walk through the jungle."

The men nodded and shifted along the wall. One pushed at his plate with a dirty boot.

"Let me show you where to sleep" my father said.

"Please, gentlemen, follow me."

Without bathing or washing the crusty bits of posho and beans from their hands, the soldiers wiped their hands on their pants, gathered up their belongings and followed him to my bedroom.

I heard a metal clank and glanced through a hole in the curtain that divided off the room. Dada was watching Gabo take the bayonet off his AK47, untie his three bullet magazines, and re-arrange them. One snapped into the gun; the others could be hooked onto it without untying the bundle.

"Patrick!" my mother hissed.

I moved away from the curtain. She shook her head at me. I pretended to be absorbed in the book on my lap, occasionally turning an unread page. All the while my ears were tuned into the hushed voices of the men behind me. Most of what was said fell to the distance between us, but occasional words made the journey: . *.freedom . . . revolt . .*

overthrow . . . They stuck in my mind like rice burned on the bottom of a cook-pot.

Shortly, Dada returned. The flickering candles lit his wide, shining eyes and cast his face in a warm glow. Though his body remained stiff with the evening's stress, the set of his jaw spoke of determination, not fear.

"These men may be the first and last hope we have," he told us. We sat quietly, casting glances at each other, as Dada moved away from the doorway and sat down in his chair. My mother was the first to break the silence.

"John, there is no way that Patrick is sleeping in his room with those rebels."

"They are not rebels, they are freedoms fighters!" Dada replied.

"Yes, they are fighters!" Mama said, her voice barely above a whisper. "And who knows what they are capable of!"

I sat silent and still. Despite my curiosity, I had no desire to sleep in that small space with those strangers, their guns, and the potent odors of war they carried with them.

"The kids can sleep in our room tonight," Dada said. He sighed, raised his hands, and then dropped them as if he was flustered by Mama's concerns. Then he looked around at all of us, and a smile spread across his face.

"The good news is, I do not have to go to Rwanda."

"How come?" Mama asked, some of the tension leaving her voice.

I leaned closer so as not to miss a word.

"I will tell you soon," Dada promised. "For now, all I can say is that something is happening, something that may change our lives for good."

*   *   *

I slept restlessly that night, waking at the slightest

rustle of wind blowing through the eucalyptus in our back yard. Shortly before dawn the voices of Gabo and his men filtered in through the curtain. My father pushed himself up quietly from the straw mat where he and mother lay and tiptoed over the sleeping forms of my siblings. Through the tattered bedroom curtain, I caught flashes of the men moving by the glow of a kerosene lamp. Dada shook hands with each of them as they slung their guns over their shoulders and hefted bulging canvas bags. Then Dada grabbed his sweater, slipped on his rubber shoes, blew out the candle, and left with the men. Darkness reclaimed the room. Soon, I drifted back to sleep.

*   *   *

When I rose with the sun to begin my pre-school chores, I found Dada already outside gathering the milking group. We herded the cows into the *kraal* with little conversation.

I was eager to know where he had gone with the men, why he no longer had to go to Rwanda, and many more details of the hushed conversations I had not been privy to. But as usual I feared he wouldn't respond well to my prying. As we sat side by side, pulling milk from the cow's swollen udders, I searched my mind for an unobtrusive way to broach the subject and came up short. Choosing the direct approach, I asked, "So, where did you and the men go this morning?"

"Not far away," he replied. "They're still around, but I can't tell you where."

My hands paused in their pulling. I remembered my mother's whispered words from the night before. "*What about the government military? Do you think they will find out they were here?*"

Dada looked over at me with hard eyes. A moment of concern fell between us.

Then he growled, "Not if you keep your mouth

shut." He grasped my arm firmly. "You didn't see anyone or hear anything last night. Do you understand me?"

I nodded slowly, shocked.

"Good. Now finish milking and get ready for school."

Igitengi *(Male shoulder-wrapping garb)*

The morning unfolded ominously. During the long walk to school, no one uttered a word as we each privately mulled the previous day's events. When we arrived, one of the school captains accused us of tardiness. Distracted and unsure of his authority, I suffered two blows beneath his cane before ripping it out of his fist. Our scuffle attracted the attention of a teacher, who stopped us. Nonetheless, the violence of the encounter poisoned the air; I couldn't focus on my studies.

When we got home, our parents were preparing

food. The guerilla fighters were nowhere to be seen, but I knew it was for them. Dada poured some milk from our ration and boiled it with tea leaves and sugar, while Mama ladled beans and boiled potatoes into plastic containers. They packed the items carefully into a large basket.

Dinner that night was meager—a cold portion of beans and milk. I eyed the overstocked basket with a rumbling stomach. Later, it disappeared with Dada.

Sleep eluded me that night, chased off by images of violence. As I lay in bed, staring into the darkness, I overheard my parents speaking in the other room.

"I'm pleased by my contribution to the rebel cause," Dada said. "I can tell you one thing, that kind of life is hard!"

"How are they?" Mama asked. "Your so-called 'trusted heroes.'"

"Dealing with the heat by day and the cold by night," Dada answered, letting out a deep sigh. "They *are* fighting for a good cause, you know."

"I know," Mama replied, her voice a mix of anxiety and admission. "Still, my insides churn when I think about the violence they bring."

"I understand, my dear," Dada soothed, "but that doesn't mean you should doubt them."

A low, but persistent rap at the door interrupted their exchange.

I lay very still. Dada must have tiptoed across the room, because the next thing I heard was the gentle unlatching of the door, followed by Dada's worried voice.

"What brings you at this late hour, Baaba?"

"Close the door first." my grandfather's words were low and firm. I rolled over and slid to a place where I could peek through a hole in the curtain that divided my room from the main one. Through the hole, I watched Baaba lift his *Igitengi* garb and lower himself onto Dada's wooden chair. My parents moved around him like a pair of nervous gazelles.

"Someone just told me they saw four armed rebels in our area," Baaba said. "Were they in this house?"

I heard Mama shifting uneasily.

"John, did the rebels come to you?" Baaba asked again.

"Yes," Dada answered reluctantly.

"See what I told you!" Mama cried, loud enough to wake everyone. Through the hole, I saw her clenched fists come down hard on her thighs. When she continued her voice was quieter but just as vehement. "Even with all this sneaking around at night, there is no way four armed men can go unnoticed in our small village."

Dada stalked around the room, a swift flash of legs, then squatted by Baaba's side and spoke to him in tones too low for me to make out. A swirl of skirts briefly obscured my view as Mama stormed towards them, sinking down to grip her husband's shoulder. "What have we done? Is it too late?" she demanded.

Dada flung out his arm, sending her rocking back. Her bottom hit the floor with a thud. "Not now, Florence!" he barked.

My heart pounded so hard I thought they would hear it. I had never seen my father treat my mother roughly.

Baaba rose slowly. I heard the rustle of him wrapping his *Igitengi* over his shoulders. Despite the darkness, I could envision the disapproval in his eyes as he said, "Treat her well, son, you're going to need her in the coming days."

"Baaba?" Mama called, as he moved towards the door. I could just make out his feet and the lower half of my mother, still on the floor. "What do we do?"

Baaba turned back towards her. He let out a deep sigh. "Be prepared for the worst. I have seen and survived such wars and they never end well."

*   *   *

As another day broke on the dawn of civil war, even the sun could not lift the shroud of darkness in our minds. We all went about our daily routines, but the ominous unknown weighted the air. Even my little sisters, too young to comprehend the events unfolding around them, acted restrained: their eyes wide and watching, their play quiet and superficial.

Just before my sisters and I set out for school, a neighbor came by and told us not to bother. Classes were canceled indefinitely.

Dada shifted nervously when I passed on the news. "Take the milk to the vending station," he said. "I need to stay behind and prepare."

"Prepare?" I asked.

"For war, Patrick."

Panda Gali (military raid)

The cool dark of the jungle and the whistling of my bicycle tires against the dirt path offered a brief respite from the searing heat of that word: *War*. Even here, in the relative comfort of old spreading pines and cactus brush, the air felt different, still and loaded. There were fewer birds, as if they'd flown deeper into the jungle to wait for violent humanity to burn itself out. Kilometers flew beneath my bike wheels, the swaying squeak of the milk-laden metal jerrycan echoed too loudly.

At the milk exchange station I joined other farmers to wait for the truck from Baale Town. It never came. As time stretched on, the men began to murmur to each other. More of those loaded words sneaked into my ears: *Death. Roadblock. Rebellion.*

Flies buzzed angrily about our sweating heads and

the faint crust of sweet milk on our metal containers.

Panda Gali. Chaos.

The sun was too high in the sky. Muttering gave way to shuffling. Finally, with quiet sighs, the farmers began to disperse, heading back to their homes, containers still heavy with milk.

Just as the last men and I were packing to go, we heard a strange sound. It wasn't the coughing and grinding of the truck, but something far lower and subtler, like the movement of cattle. We looked down the road to Baale Town. A faint cloud of dust rose in the air. From within it, a man appeared. Then another, and another, a procession of men, women, and children, shuffling silently, bowed under the weight of bulging loads, bed sheets and sisal mats wrapped tightly around the bulky bundles balanced on their heads and shoulders. As they passed by, I could see that dust caked their faces, cut through by tears or sweat or both. Babies slept where they were tied to their mother's backs. A noxious smell of waste and fear clung to the silent children who lagged behind them. Not a single person offered greeting as they passed. With lowered heads, their glazed eyes followed the cracked heels of the person before them.

Finally, Karim, a well-known farmer in our milk-selling group, broke the silence. "Muna," he called to one of the dusty-faced men, stepping off the curb to fall in beside his friend. "What is this exodus?"

Muna looked up from the road. Slowly, recognition warmed his face and relaxed his jaw. He stepped away from the slow-moving group and put down his basket.

"Karim," he said simply, shaking the farmer's hand.

"Word has not made it here yet?"

"No, friend," Karim replied. "But we've waited hours for a milk truck that never came. What's the news?"

"The NRA guerilla fighters have attacked the police post in Baale," Muna explained. "It is said they ran away with all the guns, blew up the bank in Kayunga, and took all the cash. The government militia is on their heels, and anger sharpens their steel. They will burn whatever they touch."

"Good God," Karim exclaimed. "It has begun."

*   *   *

I raced home along the rocky road, milk bottle clanking and sloshing. Gabo and his men were responsible for this; there was no doubt in my mind. The secret knowledge had burned at my throat while I stood there listening to Muna, needing to take in and commit to memory every one of his words, strip them for every detail, while at the same time itching to return home to my family and share the news.

Gabo and his men bombed and robbed the Baale bank, attacked the police station—and my family had housed and fed them. Why hadn't Gabo warned us? If they were supposed to be protecting us--why were they bringing the war here? Was this betrayal?

My legs pedaled harder as I wheezed, ached, and sweat stung my eyes. Chickens ran clucking out of my way as I cranked up to the house, skidding to a stop in a cloud of dust. As it settled, I saw a man sitting on the veranda, but it was not Dada, Baaba or one of my uncles. We had company. A brief wall rose in my mind, against which all the racing thoughts crashed into a tangled heap.

Gatare, a lanky, thin-faced Rwandese man I only knew as Dada's friend from Baale, sat stiffly on a wooden stool, watching me. His wife held a three-year-old boy on her lap, while their five-year-old son played with a toy wooden car in the dirt beside her. I greeted them with a nod, went straight into the house; still no Dada. Mama sat intently mending a cow-hide sac. Her head jerked as I entered, and relief released her tight brow. Dropping the sac, she ran to pull me into a tight embrace.

"Good. You are home and safe," she sighed.

Holding me out at arm's length, she studied my dust-darkened face and added, "You heard about what happened in Baale."

"I biked home as fast as I could to tell you and Dada."

"I see that. He is at your Baaba's house. Go speak to them; they will want to see you." She sent me off with a sad nod.

Gatare and his family sat silent and unmoving on our porch, save for the rolling squeak of the toddler's wooden toy. I breezed past them and ran the two hundred meters to Baaba's home. Dada and Baaba sat on wooden chairs in the meager shade of the grass-thatched roof. Despite the sultry season air, both men held their arms across their chests as though they were cold. The two of them turned at my approach. Baaba's face did not form into its usual smile. Instead, the corners of his thin, old mouth pulled down in an unnatural way. Dada leaned back and took his hands from his chest to clasp the back of his head wearily.

I pulled up a stool and spilled Muna's story.

"It is good you stayed to listen, son," Dada said, nodding approval. "Gatare and his family brought word of the attacks not long before you arrived. We knew this war would reach us, we just didn't think it would be so soon."

Baaba nodded affirmation and remained uncharacteristically quiet.

The thoughts I'd been holding so tight burned through.

"It was Gabo, wasn't it?" I asked.

"Yeah," Dada sighed. He shrugged, almost nonchalantly. "They needed more guns and ammunition."

"But why are they bombing and breaking into banks?" I asked. "I thought Gabo's guerillas were the good guys."

"They're stealing money to buy food, medicine, and

more guns to use in battle," Dada explained, shifting again. He leaned forward and clasped his hands before him. "In times of war, son, some things may not seem right; the end result is what matters."

I could see Baaba working his jaw in irritation, but still he did not speak. He seemed tired and old, as if he'd done all he could, and now he had to let his son take the lead, despite the consequences. Dada shifted under the presumed responsibility. His eyes flew to Baaba, seeking reassurance, then back to me.

"Does that mean we are safe?" I asked.

"No!" Baaba said suddenly.

I was glad to hear him speak, but the unfamiliar cut of his tone shocked me.

"Father!" Dada said, too loud. His eyes widened and fixed on the old man.

Baaba sat up straight and shook his head. "Rwabagabo should know the situation as it is. He is old enough and needs to understand the danger we are in."

A terrible silence hung over us. I used the quiet moment to gather my thoughts and speak my mind. "I know things are bad," I said. "But there must be good coming from all this, right? Gabo, the rebels, they are fighting to protect us, aren't they?"

"That is what your grandfather and I were discussing when you arrived."

"What we know," Baaba began, settling back into the chair, "is that Gabo is our own, and the guerilla group has over ten thousand men and women. Out of those, there are over one thousand Rwandese Tutsi fighters with high rank. I believe that they, being our kind, will not betray us."

"Patrick, war is a complicated thing," my father added. "Even though the freedom fighters are on our side, it doesn't mean that they can protect us individually. They are fighting to protect the entire nation of Tutsi, not just our family."

Baaba's eyes narrowed. He added, "These guerillas—the NRA—are a small group with little money going up against our big, bribe-fattened government. Before they can attempt to capture power, they must move quietly throughout the country, little by little taking over or destroying the government's resources. The government will chase them. They will send out Special Forces to kill anyone who might aid the rebels. Their bullets will not discriminate." He paused to wipe his mouth, directing a hard look at my father.

Dada studied the horizon, clamped his mouth shut, and pretended not to notice grandpa's glare.

Baaba continued, "Along the way, they will rape and pillage for pleasure. Good may come from this, Rwabagabo. If the NRA overthrows the government, it will mean an end to political discrimination against Ugandan Tutsi. But we are not safe, not until this is over. Wherever our rebels go, the war will follow."

Seven

September, 1984 (Baale, Uganda)

Icubahiro *(Customary respect)*

The next day, the sun burned the dew off the grass the same as it had the morning before. The cows lazily chewed their cud as we milked them. The thin streams of creamy liquid echoed the same melody into our metal pails. Day began with all the sounds, sights, smells and movements of every morning of my life; in the stillness of the moment, it was as if nothing had changed.

But then, in an instant, nothing was the same. Our family was no longer thinking, talking and worrying about war, we were preparing for war.

Mama bustled about, putting necessities and precious items into baskets that could be gathered in a moment's notice. Dada and I didn't pour off any milk to sell. There was no one to buy it, and we would need all the food we could get. Gatare's family remained with us, and more people trickled into our care as the conflict zone widened. They'd been chased out of their homes and arrived at ours with little money or anything else. We sheltered them and shared our dwindling supplies. A week ago, visitors would have meant boisterous discussions and the guzzling of *waragi*, children chasing each other and the chickens with squeals of joy, and the chatter of women as they cooked. Even the toddlers dug quietly in the dirt. An eerie, fear-fueled quiet hung over our household.

Somewhere amid the low bustle of breakfast activity, Dada sought me out. He told me to follow him back to the main house. We walked past the visitors who lounged near the kitchen hut. He motioned me to wait outside and disappeared briefly, the door squeaking behind him. A minute later, he reappeared with a metal suitcase.

"Let's go," he said, jerking his head in the direction

of the jungle.

"We need to hide this. Keep your head down and your eyes open."

We moved quickly out of the trampled yard and into the surrounding wilderness. The canopy overhead cut off the exposing sun, and head-high brush closed around us. Once we'd gone ten meters into the protective cover of the jungle, Dada paused and motioned silence. For a long minute we stood, unmoving. Reassured by the rustling quiet that we had no followers, he nodded and led us on with an easier stride.

"What's in the case?" I finally asked, keeping my voice low.

"Money," Dada answered. "The government forces will be here soon. We will have to go into hiding for a bit, and we will have to do it quickly."

He shot me a glance. "It may be that the Special Forces merely sift through our things, decide there is nothing worth stealing, and that is the end of it. But there is also the chance that they will seize control of the area and keep it under their 'surveillance.' If that is the case, it could be a long time before we can return. We'll need this money to survive while we wait for the NRA to win our freedom." He spat angrily into the thorny mess of an apple of Sodom bush.

"But can't we just take the money with us when we leave? Why do we need to hide it?"

"There is a small chance we will not have time to take anything with us when we leave, son. We may only have time to run."

*　　　*　　　*

We passed through a clearing and entered another thick forest. Dada counted fifty steps straight ahead, and then fifty to his left. I followed his tracks, then his eyes as he took in every tree, bush, and rock. There was a reason Dada had brought me along, even if he did not voice it. I needed to know this hiding place as well as he did. Just in case. I drew the landscape in my memory. Then, following Dada's lead, I grabbed a stick. Together we dug a hole beside a wild fig tree. We buried the case and covered it with vines and ferns.

As we made our way back home, we covered our tracks by scuffing dirt and fluffing the grass behind us. Dada paused several times to survey the area with a penetrating gaze.

When we arrived home, one of the displaced families was gone.

"They went north," Mama said. "They plan to cross the Nile and head to a safe district."

Dada's brow furrowed and his eyes darkened with thought, as if he were contemplating whether we should follow.

Inside the house a baby cried. Gatare emerged,

clutching a glass of frothy milk in both hands as if it were the last thing he'd ever hold. He sank onto a bench beneath the mulberry tree, put down the milk, and leaned his forearms on his thighs. "John," he said, squeezing the bridge of his nose. "Do you foresee an end to this?"

"No," Dada said firmly. "This is just the beginning."

He sat down next to Gatare on the bench and looked off towards Baale town.

"Patrick," he ordered, without shifting his gaze. "Head to Misanga and buy food. Florence, give him a list of what we'll need to feed everyone."

Mama's face went slack. I didn't know if it was with fear of spending what little we had feeding so many mouths, or because he was sending me out alone while war waxed around us—or which of these threats I should be more concerned about. She took me aside as the men fell into conversation. She gave me money.

I rode my bicycle quickly down the path with the same hyperawareness for any shifts in the surrounding jungle that I had the first time I'd traveled it—the first day I attended Mr. Rueben's Village School. Back then, I'd carried a fear of the animals that haunted the dark shadows; now, it was for traces of other humans that my senses were primed—it was for the government and their Special Forces. As I rode into Misanga, the solemn faces of villagers tending their homes and gossiping in hushed voices about the war did little to calm my worry.

At a small garden set into a farmer's wide front yard, I paid for two sacks of cassava. Unlike at the market, where we filled our bags from towering piles, here I had to harvest the roots myself. After I handed over the money, the farmer lent me a hoe and I set to work.

I'd barely unearthed half a sack when my father's voice startled me.

"We need to go, that will be enough," he said

hastily.

"What are you doing here?" I asked, dropping the hoe and pushing myself up from where I squatted in the dirt. "Did I take too long?"

"No, son. The Special Forces have arrived. We need to go." He hefted the half-full potato bag onto his bike. Streams of sweat lined his face, flowing down to his chin. I knew he had ridden hard to get to me.

We walked our bikes quickly through the soft earth of the cassava field to reach the main road. "We can't go home," Dada instructed. "Ride to Kassim's house. I will be right behind you."

I knew the route well, and started off without hesitation, standing up on my pedals to gain momentum. Dada rode quietly behind me; I had to keep casting glances back to make sure he was still there. Once we crested a big hill and wound into more protected landscape, Dada fell in beside me and our pace slowed. "Where is the rest of the family?" I asked.

"They are hiding in the jungle not too far from our home," he said, adding reluctantly, "But your Baaba is stubborn, he—."

"What do you mean, stubborn?"

"When we heard that the Special Forces were going door to door through the village, we asked him to hide with us. He refused. As we rushed into the bush, I saw him sit down in his chair and light his pipe."

"Dada, you abandoned Baaba?" I shouted, my ire rising, an untamable anger overpowering *Icubahiro*, the customary calm respect I showed him. My peddling slowed.

"Don't ever shout at me like that again, boy," Dada warned, steel in his voice. "Your Baaba refused."

A part of me split off, like a leaf that flutters from its branch. Away from me, Baaba sat sprawled in his wooden chair, warm and quiet in the sun as he waited for the Special Forces to come and kill him. Perhaps I would never see him again. Quiet fell between us as we peddled along the sandy road. Dada didn't speak again until we crested another hill and the home of his old friend came into view.

"I want you to stay with Kassim's family for a while until we have a better understanding of the situation," Dada said as we leaned our bicycles against *a mweso* seed tree.

"People believe these maniac Special Forces will go on a rampage and do all sorts of evil things."

"What evil things?" I asked.

"Rape, murder, torture. We don't have time to talk about it now, son." Dada shook his head.

"Won't the guerilla group protect us? You said they include many of our own people, and that they are a strong force."

"They are, but that is not how guerilla warfare

works."

"How does it work?"

"They must put their energy into collecting resources and fighters now. When they have overthrown the government, they will protect us," Dada explained.

"So until then, they leave us to the wrath of the Special Forces?" I asked.

Ignoring me, Dada pointed, "Look! Here's Kassim."

The stubby, bald-headed man waddled towards us. Between his hands he wrung a faded gold *kofia,* a traditional Islamic hat. "Hello, brother," he called, waving at us with the crumbled hat. His voice came out with a squeak—more like that of a boy at puberty than a fifty-five-year-old man.

"Hello, Al-Hadji Kassim," Dada answered.

"Patrick, you are drenched in sweat," Kassim noted, his own bright cotton frock stained with dark swoops beneath the armpits and circling his neck. "Do you need a glass of water?"

"No, thank you," I answered.

"I'm sure you've heard what's going on in Baale town," Dada said.

Kassim nodded this solemnly, and led us towards his home. A large banana grove surrounded the thatched hut, and his twelve children played noisily in the shaded yard. Dada left me with them while he and Kassim stepped away to talk out of our earshot.

The men returned with faces lowered and humorless. "You are going to stay here until things settle down in Baale," Dada instructed me. "It is ten kilometers from the city, and with Kassim you are safe. I will come back as soon as I find out what will become of our town and village. Okay, Patrick?"

"Okay," I answered, not really meaning it. I was afraid I would end up waiting a long time.

Hefting the half-full bag of cassava onto his bicycle, Dada took off down the road. Kassim instructed his kids to find me something to eat and went back out to where Dada and I had first seen him. He wrung the *kofia* in his restless hands.

While Kassim's oldest son and I ate bananas and practiced bicycle tricks, the old man paced the driveway, talking about the war with everyone that passed by. Occasionally, he paused from talking to duck inside and pack sacks of beans, rice, and other foods. I didn't have to ask why.

By the time my father returned, the sun had begun its retreat, allowing the air to cool and the sweat to finally dry to a sticky itch on my skin. Dada rode in at a pace more fitting to his calm and deliberate nature, but stress still haunted his face.

"What is the situation, brother?" Kassim asked, with a faint smile.

"Mmm . . . maybe better," Dada said, chewing on the words as though he was not sure. "I don't think better is the right word," he corrected. "The situation has stabilized for the moment."

"Clarify for me, brother," Kassim prodded.

"The rebels retreated and the government troops moved into Baale. For now, they're telling people they are there to protect them and they should report immediately any knowledge of rebel activity or whereabouts."

"Ha!" Kassim spat. He looked down at the ground, etching a complex pattern through the dirt with a bare toe. "Lying skunks! They will 'protect' us from themselves until they have the information they need, and then . . .." He swiped his foot across the dirt, destroying the design.

"I know," my father concurred, shaking his head. "But we are back in our homes for the moment, as are other families in our village. Hopefully this will buy us a few days."

He turned to me. "Get your bicycle. We don't have time to waste."

Twihishe *(Let us hide)*

When I got home, my mother and sisters greeted me with long embraces. Their faces wore the strain of the long day spent hiding in the woods, fear for their own and each other's lives present with every carefully drawn breath. None of them, not even the toddlers, played or laughed. They sat quietly in the dirt beside my mother, dusty tear stains marking their faces. "*Twihishe*," "we hid," is all they would say.

Giving distracted answers to concerns about my health and my stay at Kassim's, I hurried out to check on Baaba. I found him stretched out in a hammock, puffing his pipe. For all the fear and tears and nerves of everyone else, Baaba seemed as cloaked in serenity as he was in smoke.

His arms dangled into the grass, and his legs crossed lazily at the ankles. When he saw me, he lifted his head a bit, then leaned back comfortably.

"How did you do at Kassim's, Rwabagabo?" Baaba asked. "I was so worried about you."

"Worried about me! I was worried about you more!" I cried, fighting the urge to disturb his repose with a hug. "What would you have done if the Special Forces had come to our home? And how could you stay when everybody else ran away?"

"I am not afraid anymore, Rwabagabo," Baaba replied, waving a hand dismissively and shifting to a more comfortable position. "My biggest concern is for my children's and grandchildren's safety." He paused, adding with a sigh, "No one seems to have control over their military."

"Maybe Gabo's men will come and help," I offered. "Don't you think so, Baaba?"

"Eh . . ." he shrugged. "We can hope. But what kind of force leaves its people in the jaws of ruthless government troops? And don't get me started on that nephew of mine. Gabo has always been a loser. He failed his marriage, sold his herd, and traded his mother's cows for alcohol. When you see him with a gun, don't be fooled and think he has changed." Baaba's withered face wrinkled even more. He sat up with a grunt and grabbed his walking stick. "Come Rwabagabo; help me herd these wild calves into their *kraal*."

"Where is Uncle Kafuuko?" I asked as we walked to the pasture. The bright yellow day had given way to a bloody dusk, painting the swaying grasses in the colors of kings and battle.

"Kafuuko is not back from hiding. What a coward son he is!"

Dada materialized out of nowhere and fell into steps beside us.

"Father," he grunted.

"John!" Baaba looked over at him, surprised.

"I was coming to get Patrick to start milking." He cleared his throat. "And I heard you belittle Gabo and his men."

"They haven't given me any reason to trust them," Baaba said. "They must be crazy or stupid to believe they can raid the government like that and then leave us here unprotected from the retaliation! They know very well what will happen, but they put us in this position anyway."

"They don't have enough men to resist the government yet," Dada answered irritably. "They are doing what they must do to gain strength and amass supplies."

"And we will be the ones who suffer the consequences," Baaba said bitterly.

"Is this really about the NRA? Or is it your dislike for Gabo?" Dada asked.

"Don't patronize me," Baaba warned.

"I'm sorry, but you seem hell bent on condemning these fighters before they have the chance to prove themselves!"

Baaba pulled to a stop and turned to face his son. His words came out hard and uncompromising: "Your unfettered faith will get us all killed."

Yapfuye*(he's dead)*

The boom of a cannon shook the air. I felt the ground quake. A young voice stifled a scream. Everyone ducked and the children started to sob. My mother fell to the earth, clutching my baby brother to her breast.

"Please, stay calm," my father said, loud enough to be heard over the din of panic. "The sound is from the east, and several kilometers from here. We are safe."

His words were a shaky and superficial salve, but the only one we had. 'Safe' was the last thing any of us felt, but we quieted quickly all the same. Discovery meant rape, mutilation, murder –all those horrendous acts my father had warned me awaited those suspected of supporting the NRA. We numbered among those supporters, and even if none of our neighbors disclosed this to the Special Forces, the mere fact that we were Tutsi condemned us anyway.

Earlier that morning, my father received news that government forces were coming to search the homes in our neighborhood. We hurriedly threw our already packed bags of food and other necessities onto our backs. My mother and I gathered my eight siblings and walked into the jungle, not knowing if we'd ever return. Two other families fell in to alongside us as we followed Dada deep into the jungle, painfully leaving our dear dog Nyabwangu behind. Dada worried that the dog would give away our hiding place.

We gathered beneath the cover of a dense stand of dogbane. A faint breeze stirred the heat and sweat ran down our bodies and made the children's clothes cling with the dark loam of the forest floor. While the younger ones napped or poked about in the dirt, the adults monitored the shadows with tired eyes and talked of the war.

My father, the de facto leader of our group, walked in circles, took deep breaths, and rubbed his head constantly. He folded his arms across his chest and then loosened them. It was clear that responsibility weighed on him heavily.

"Is there anything I can do to help?" I asked.

"Sure," he answered. "See if there is any milk left for those kids." He gestured towardsthe tree where nearly thirty children too young to care for themselves napped or played quietly. There were so many mouths to feed. Mama paced about she barely breathed.

"Mama says they can't have it all at once."

"She is right," Dada said, leaning on a thick vine twisting into the canopy above. He closed his eyes and squeezed the bridge of his nose between his thumb and forefinger. "The day is still young; who knows where we will end up."

"There must be something I can do."

"I wish there were, son."

He continued to pace. I stood, waiting for his silence to break.

Finally, with a quick glance and a jerk of his head, he strode back towards where the other two men in the group stood talking. I followed close behind. Their eyes rose to meet us and their voices stilled immediately upon our arrival.

"Friends, it is coming on afternoon," my father announced, clearing his throat when his voice cracked.

"It is time to determine whether it is safe to return to our homes. If not, we will need water and more food if we can find it."

"Aren't we close to the River Nile, John?" asked Kazungu, a tall neighbor with a long nose and big drooping eyes.

"We are," Dada replied. "But we can't actually draw water. There is a swamp blocking us."

"Could we take the families to the place where you and I watered the cows during the drought?" I asked.

"No," Dada said. "It is an obvious place for the army to look for us."

He took a deep breath. My mother and the other two women drifted over to listen; sleeping babies wrapped on their hips.

"I know this jungle very well, so I'll be the fastest at gathering supplies and information. Stay here," Dada said. "I'll return as fast as I can. You should be safe, but if you do need to flee, head towards where the sun rises."

While waiting for Dada to return, I sat apart from the group, thinking about Baaba back at our house. Once again, the old man had refused to leave with us, swearing he would never again flee from his home. As much as his stubbornness frustrated me, his bravery only deepened my respect.

A few hours later, Dada reappeared with a bulging burlap sack on his shoulder. Wordlessly, he set down the heavy load, leaned against the ragged trunk of an old oak, and opened the buttons of his sweat-soaked shirt. We crowded around him like calves at a feeding trough.

"Well, I got the food and water, but . . ,"

He hesitated and cast a glance towards the children who had begun to trickle in.

"I also have sad news. Remember Muvunyi's son, who used to buy our milk?"

"Mariko?" Mama asked.

"He's been shot. *Yapfuye*, he's dead."

In the silence that followed Dada's words, Mama and Kazungu's wife made choking sounds and began to cry. Wide-eyed children clung onto their skirts, staring up with confusion.

I felt a tap on my shoulder. "There's something I need to discuss with you, son. Your mother must hear this also."

My mother wiped her face and took deep breaths as Dada led us away from the group. When he stopped and turned to us, I saw a thin film shining his eyes. It was the closest I'd ever seen my father to tears, and it deepened the waves of fear and sadness coursing through my body.

He drew in air, then examined the bushes suspiciously, avoiding eye contact. "Patrick, we have to send you away for a little while."

"We have to what?" Mama asked, her voice suddenly strong and clear. Obviously, she had not been part of making this decision.

"From what I've heard—I think Patrick will be safer in the Busoga region..."

"Are you sure?" Mama demanded. "What district is not affected by this war, John? And why is he not safer here, with us?" She grabbed my arm, pulling me close.

"Florence," Dada said, "Hold yourself together. The villagers have assured me that there is no war to the east—not yet. And I have been told that the Special Forces are targeting men and boys his age, because . . .." He shook his head and used the tails of his still-opened shirt to wipe sweat and tears from his face. "Because the government is claiming that the NRA is an army made up of boys. He is not safe so close to the conflict."

There was too much for me to take in. Thoughts tangled in my head. All I could do was try to push them aside and focus my mind on Dada. He was our leader.

"When do you want me to leave?" I asked.

"Immediately," Dada answered. "You'll head across the Nile . . . You will be safe. I . . . I assure you!" He turned sideways to hide his emotion. Though I could tell this decision had not been easy for him to make, my mind could not comprehend the details.

Panic caught me as his instructions sunk in. "I have to cross the Nile? I don't even know how to swim!"

"You will not have to swim, son," Dada said, offering a slight smile. "You will get a boat. You'll be safe."

I turned to Mama, but she kept her gaze on Dada.

"Patrick, give us a moment, please," he said.

Dada reached for her arm and rubbed it gently as he led her aside. Fear and confusion swelled within me in the slowly ticking minutes of waiting. I tried to fix my mind on the mica-flecked boulders that were scattered in the jungle, catching the sun in shards of gold, but the impossibilities of the task ahead overwhelmed me.

When my parents returned, Mama's tears were flowing. She wiped them carefully and steadied her voice.

"I guess you should go," she said. "Your father wants to make sure that one of you will be safe."

"This doesn't make sense, Mama," I said. "When do

I come back? How will I get there? Who—"

"Don't worry, son," Dada interrupted. He put his hand around my shoulder in a rare expression of affection. "I will tell you all you need to know. I guarantee you, you will be safe." He spoke the reassuring phrase as if trying to convince not only me, but himself as well. He turned me to face him. "Patrick Kalenzi, you are the only man in this family besides me. I want to make sure that if something happens to me you will carry on the family name. This group," he motioned towards the others, the thirty noisy children, the five adults, "is too big. Loud. Slow-moving. The government forces are closing in and—alone, you can move quickly, you can *kwihisha*, hide quietly. You are fast, and clever," he said. Squatting down beside me, he smoothed the dirt with his hand and began to draw a map.

Eight

April, 1985 (Misanga, Uganda)

Umuhizi*(the hunter)*

No moisture softened the earth beneath my feet. No papyrus swamps overtook the thick jungle. No smells of rotting vegetation greeted my nose. I'd been hiking for hours, but there was no sign of the Nile.

I quickened my pace, breaking into a run. Underbrush sliced my legs. I felt the pain but it only drove me on faster. My lungs burned. Sweat stung my eyes. Each twig that cracked under my feet sounded like an explosion. Ahead, another open space beckoned. I ran harder, hoping that this was the break in the savannah that would give way to river-lining swamps. Thorny bushes tall as a man formed a thin fence around it. They tore red streaks across my numb legs and arms as I wrestled my way through.

It was just another clearing, backed by yet another forest. A fat mango tree, usually only found near homesteads, stood like a sentinel near its center. I paused in its shade to let my thoughts settle.

I was tired, hungry, and thirsty, but carried little food and had no idea when I'd find water. The few crumpled bills in my pocket offered no consolation—I had not seen a single person or village since leaving my family. My father's maps, swiftly memorized, had long ago dissolved into uselessness as I walked in circles, passing the same landmark after hours of wandering. Dehydration and disorientation muddled my thoughts and blurred my vision. I had no idea which way to go. The only thing I could do was close my eyes and pray for an idea to come.

Suddenly, a low growl sounded from behind me. I whipped my head around and saw a feral-looking man with a large knife strapped on, dressed only in disintegrating cotton shorts. He brandished a spear. Two large, muscular dogs flanked him, their lips curled in angry snarls.

The man stopped a stone's throw away. "Don't move, boy," he hissed, and I could smell the odor of his rotting mouth. "Or I'll let the dogs loose!"

I froze, hands spread out at my sides in a gesture of innocence. The bushman snapped his fingers and came towards me, the dogs matching his stride. I searched the surrounding jungle for any way to escape. All I saw was the same homogonous enclosure of green shadows I'd found before.

"*Kachini*," the bushman commanded, pulling to a stop before me. His dogs sank obediently to their haunches. I wondered if I should do the same.

A strong odor of smoke and sweat from him provoked a wave of nausea. He peered at me, his eyes small and hard like black peas embedded in leathery folds of skin. Long clumps of matted hair twisted around his bony face.

"What are you doing here?" he demanded.

I searched my mind for the story Dada instructed me to offer strangers. "I am gathering firewood?"

"You are trespassing on my hunting area. Where are you from?"

"I . . . live in the next village," I almost choked on the lie.

"The next village? That is simply not true!"

"What do you mean it's not true?"

"In that direction," he said, pointing north, "is the river."

"Head this way," he continued, now pointing West. "All you will find is a couple of farms. To your left is a village: my village. The only village for many miles. And I have never seen you before."

"You've never seen me?"

"I don't have time for your games." The dogs panted at his side, big teeth glinting in the sun. I did not foresee being able to outrun them anywhere, let alone in the hunting grounds where they'd likely lived their entire lives.

"All right," I sighed, pulling my hands up to hide my face. "I'm from a small village of Kiyange, near Baale,"

"Baale? You are this far from your home? What are you doing in this jungle?"

"I'm lost. Like you say, I shouldn't be here. I should be at the river Nile, but I can't find it."

"Why do you need to—," a bit of concern replaced the aggression in his tone.

"Can you please tell me how to get to the river Nile?" I interjected.

"That's easy; go straight that way," he said, pointing west. "Why do you need to go to the river at this hour?"

"Sir, I can't return home."

"But why?"

The very things about this man that terrified me also served to assure me that he had no affiliations with the Special Forces. Honest words tumbled from me. "Because the rebels attacked Baale police station and the government has sent its military in retaliation, and now they are terrorizing the villages looking for the rebels, and my whole family and many people from my village and Baale have gone into hiding in the jungle."

I took a deep gasp of air. "My father thinks I will be safer across the Nile," I added with a dubious shrug.

Umuhizi, the hunter, let the butt of his spear rest on the ground as astonishment softened his voice and face. "Well, that is really bad," he said. "I didn't know there had been attacks so close by. I will help you get to the river. Just wait while I check my nets."

As much as the idea of a personal guide sounded

appealing, the dogs and the tangled mess of a beard hanging over the hunter's bare chest made me hesitate. What I wanted was to get away as quickly as possible, preferably in the direction of the Nile. "You said it was that way, right?" I asked pointing north. "Then, I should be able to get there easily. Thank you!"

The bushman laughed. "Further on there are as many paths as a mouse leaves trails. You will wind up taking the wrong one." He shook his head and turned away. "Just wait here. I will show you the way."

The hunter returned laden with his nets, which he carried over his shoulders as we wound a narrow path out of the jungle. A wide savanna opened, carpeted with swaying spear-grass so high that the dogs nearly disappeared in it, their ears poking up here and there when something caught their attention. A little ways on, bracken fern, palms, and papyrus began to appear. The sight sent a quiver of hope through me. We passed over a hill, and a magnificent body of water laid itself out before us, shining like a golden mirror in the evening sun.

"That is the River Nile," the hunter said.

"That?" I replied, incredulous. "It's huge. Are you sure this is not Lake Kyoga?"

"The Nile has many sections that are wider than a lake, but that doesn't make it one."

The closer we got to the water, the more daunting the task of crossing it seemed. Not a single boat speckled its vast expanse.

A hut appeared off to our left, and then another.

"This is the fishing bay," the hunter said. "You should find a sailor here to take you across."

Our path wound closer to the river bank, past more grass-thatched huts and small gardens of overgrown plants crossed over here and there with clotheslines. Palms rose ragged and molting from the damp earth and fish hung drying from the occasional tin roof. Scrawny chickens scratched at the dirt and with gentle clucks; a door creaked in the wind. An eerie feeling tickled the back of my neck. Save the chickens, the town was empty of life.

A furious eruption of barking interrupted the ghostly quiet.

The hunter took off towards the sound, and I followed close on his heels. We dashed between houses and ducked under clotheslines to emerge on a sandy shoreline cluttered with deadwood and rotting fishing refuse. Near one dank heap, the hunter's dogs raged against a shaggy blond mutt.

"Muyizi, let go, let go now!"

The hunter wrestled the dogs apart, and the mutt took off, squealing like a baby pig. He disappeared between the huts. The hunter's dogs padded off to rummage through another rotting pile. Quiet returned.

"Where do you suppose everybody is?" I asked.

Kicking up sand with a bare foot, the hunter gazed

out at the fishing boats anchored offshore, bobbing emptily on the water.

"Usually, this time of day, there are many people here. They are drinking after a day on the river, or going out to lay nets for the night. This is all very strange."

"So how should I cross to Busoga? I expected to be there tonight."

"I do not know, my friend," he answered.

We walked along the shore, the smell of rotting fish bringing tears to my eyes and a burning sensation to my nostrils. It was the only thing strong enough to break through my anxiety.

"I wonder if the military came here already?" the hunter mused, seemly unaffected by the putrid odor.

"I imagine that is the reason everyone left." He continued to talk himself before I could reply. "If the military were in Baale, they probably came here as well. Or they are on their way, and the people here knew it and ran away." He stopped before a cluster of small houses and turned to study me. "Much like you and your family did."

"You may be right," I replied. *You will be safe* my father had repeated before I left, over and over. But nothing about this situation felt safe, nothing about it felt right. This place was alien and deserted; judging by the half-full nets of dead fish, the swinging doors, the laundry still hanging on the lines; it had been deserted in a rush of panic. My eyes took in a landscape that bore signs of war worse than where I'd run from. But how could my father have known what he was sending me into? My homeland had become an unpredictable and angry beast.

"Listen," the hunter said. "I do not think you will make it across the Nile tonight."

"I guess not."

"So what are you going to do?" he asked.

The receding sun stole its dim light from the empty village. A single Crested Crane pecked on a heap of garbage in the distance, and it occurred to me that I too was now a scavenger.

"I don't know yet, but I will have to find a way."

I watched the crane. If only, like him, I had wings to carry me across the river.

"I'm going to head home," the hunter said. "But should you feel like coming with me, it would be fine."

I squinted at the unkempt man, still weary of his intention. I had never been given anything for free from a stranger—except for contempt and beatings. The crane, picking at the garbage, could swallow poison and die. Who knew what would happen if I followed this man to his house? No, I would be safer here, alone with the rotting fish.

"Thank you, but I'll stay here tonight. Perhaps a boatman will come by early in the morning, and I can catch a ride with him."

"Do as you like," the hunter said, spreading his

hands wide like someone conceding an argument. He turned into the last rays of sunlight and walked away with his dogs.

I wandered down the shore, casting my eyes about for any sign of life or hope. An upside-down fishing boat lay canted in the sand. I sat on it and surveyed the growing night. Above me, stars began to flicker. I needed to find a place to sleep before darkness left me blind.

The houses at the end of the bay appeared more protected from the main road, and offered faster access to both the river and the swamps. Should a quick escape be necessary, they seemed the best option. Ignoring the protests of my travel-weary legs, I headed towards them.

A hand-woven mat, its colors faded by night and age, lay neatly centered on a veranda tucked behind a stone building. The small sign of order comforted me. I pushed it against the wall of the house and sank down, exhausted. With my knees drawn to my chin and arms wrapped tight around my legs, I waited for the night to be over.

*   *   *

Darkness still owned the fish harbor when I awoke, shivering. A steady wind stirred the star-sparked waters of the Nile and passed easily through the thin cotton of my shirt. I stood up, rubbing my arms and stomping my numb feet. The door to the house looked flimsy and loose. I gave it a push. Locked, but not very securely. As I gathered my strength to give it another heave, a man's loud voice stopped me short.

"Hello there, young man, are you still here?" It was the hunter, confirmed by a bark from his dog.

In the empty chill of the night, there was something comforting in his voice, something almost fatherly. I called back, "Hello! Is something wrong, sir?"

"No, I came to get you."

"To get me?"

"Sempa can't simply leave you in such a place," he said, introducing himself for the first time. "You will be able to return when the sun is up and we will look for ways to cross the Nile."

The concern in his voice was clear and honest. My lingering distrust disappeared with the next cool gust of wind. I followed my new friend and his dogs past the huts onto a dirt path. The night had never seemed so disorienting. Perhaps it was exhaustion, perhaps hunger, perhaps the lack of moon in the star-washed sky. We wound through the swamps, across swaths of grass, and back into the forest. Keeping my head down to still the waves of confusion, I followed blindly on Sempa's silent heels.

I don't know how long we walked; it could have been minutes or miles. The dark world held the soft mystery of a dream. At some point, the ground ahead began to take on a curious red glow. I looked up to see a small hut, its door open to reveal the glowing coals of a fire pit. The shack's walls hung unfinished and holes dotted its grass roof, but for all its crudeness, the place felt welcoming—a crimson heart beating quietly amid the lurking dark body of the jungle.

"Welcome to my home," Sempa said, beckoning me inside.

"Thank you, sir," I replied. The air inside the house felt warm and alive. It smelled faintly of smoked meat and burnt potatoes. The coals painted everything in soft warmth and red.

"I realize I didn't formally introduce myself. I'm SempaSeguya, but please call me Sempa."

"Thank you, I'm Patrick Kalenzi."

"Patrick . . . a white man's name. Why?"

"My parents took me for baptism. They thought I should have a Christian name."

"Do you believe in God?" Sempa asked.

"Yes, and I have spent a lot of time praying to him since I started my journey."

Sempa met my humor with a smile, then glanced around at his meager possessions. There was not much, just a roughly-made stool and a few plastic utensils poking from a plastic jug. He reached into a corner and produced a thick animal hide. "Here," he said, handing it to me. "Sit on this. I will be back shortly with food." With that, he disappeared out the open doorway

Outside, I could hear him breaking branches and twigs to make a fire. The odors intensified, eliciting painful growls from my stomach. The wait for dinner couldn't have been long, but sleep stole me in empty blinks of escape from the troubled world.

Then, Sempa was shaking me awake, a steaming plate in his hand. The flavors of the food were rich and gamey; dark stewed meat and *posho*, cornbread.

Sempa did not eat, but moved in and out of the

house, like a bee from its hive. I became accustomed to the odd rhythm of our conversation and the interludes of chirping crickets. At some point I paused to ask what kind of meat I was eating.

My host smiled. "Does it matter?" he replied.

I continued devouring the steaming stew. In my mind, I called it antelope.

"Why do you live so far from other people?" I asked, as my hunger began to wane, replaced with curiosity about my strange host.

"What do you mean?"

"It's quite lonely. Do you have neighbors?"

"Why is that important to you?" Sempa asked, cocking his head.

I studied his expression, wondering if perhaps my prying bothered him. This war had created uncertainty amongst people; neighbor and family alike turned each other in to the government militia out of hate, to save their own life, or for other unknown reasons. But Sempa didn't seem paranoid or guarded.

"No, I don't have neighbors. I like it this way," Sempa answered with a shrug, and stepped out the door.

When he walked back in I asked, "Does your village have its own name?"

"Yes, it's called Misanga. What is yours called?"

"Mine is called Kiyange, which is part of Baale Sub-County," I said.

"Kiyange? Who are your parents?" Sempa asked. "I know some people in that area. I occasionally go by the trading center in your village on my way to Baale, when I have to do shopping, or to pay my graduated government tax."

"My father's name is John Kafuniza," I answered. "Do you know him?"

"Not personally, but . . . I think I know his brothers! I have seen them at a bar. His brothers are there almost every time I visit," Sempa laughed.

"That's typical of my uncles!" I smiled, amused and disturbed by the notoriety of their drinking.

"So, feel at home now that we know each other," he offered. "And don't worry; we will be safe here from the military forces."

"How can you be so sure?" I asked.

"I have been told that they go mostly for rich families or those with many females. I obviously do not fit either category. However, it is not as safe in the village. We should leave early tomorrow to find some way for you to cross the Nile."

Taking my empty plate, the hunter disappeared outside. I watched the red glow of the coals fade. A feeling of safety and satiety softened the darkness around me. As I finally succumbed to sleep, I caught a few words; Sempa saying to me or his dogs how happy he was that he knew my uncles.

* * *

I woke up in the same spot where I ate my dinner. A dream lingered in my mind--images of myself waiting at the river bank, government militia dressed in green camouflage appearing out of the vegetation to surround me. My mouth tasted of fear, hard and metallic as their guns.

Cupping the back of my head, I leaned against the rough wall of the shack. Cobwebs and the black soot of burnt kerosene coated its low ceiling, faintly illuminated by the spreading dawn. What darkness lay ahead? The ghost town haunted my memory. Dada would never have sent me here if he'd known what I'd find. What if he was also wrong about the Busoga region? What if it was no less war-torn than it was here?

My mind wandered back to images of my father, pulling at his hair and pacing. Just to find food for my mother and eight siblings seemed a daunting enough task, and I'd left him alone to shoulder the responsibility of caring for three families. He'd made the choice to send me off hastily, without even consulting my mother. What if it was the wrong choice? What if my family needed me?

The hunter poked his head into the still-open door. His face was as black as the ceiling, his eyes wide and clear as if he'd been up for hours.

"Hello, sir," I greeted him.

"Hello Patrick Kalenzi!" He replied. "Dawn is breaking. We should leave soon to avoid the government's army."

I hesitated for a moment. The dream flashed through my head again, images of soldiers surrounding me, guns raised. Another image pushed in--my family, in the jungle, also surrounded, my mother trying to soothe my crying siblings before the ruthless soldiers quieted them forever. Then I thought of Baaba, strong and stubborn, calmly smoking his pipe, never leaving his home.

"I'm very grateful for your hospitality, but I must go find my family."

"Must find your family? What about crossing the Nile?"

"This situation is not right. Had my father known what I would find here, he would not have sent me." I paused, then continued, "I cannot abandon my family on the small chance it might save my own life. We are a small force against such a terrible power. We must stick together, stand our ground, protect each other." The thoughts formed as they left my mouth, but the words felt right.

"Can you wait for breakfast? I can make it quickly."

"No, thank you," I answered. "When peace returns, I will come back and visit you. Then we can enjoy breakfast together."

"Please do. I admire your courage and loyalty, Patrick Kalenzi. You are welcome here anytime."

Sempa led me towards a clearing, and pointed the way back to my village. He described how to keep the sun at my shoulder so I wouldn't get lost, and showed me how to study the way the moss grew on the trees to help find my direction should clouds come to cover my guiding star. I thanked him again for his hospitality and guidance and headed back into the woods.

This time the path was easier. I moved faster with every step, finally breaking into a jog. Many feelings competed for attentionfueling an awful anxiety. Returning home against my father's wishes stirred fear of his anger, while having abandoned them in the first place stirred guilt. Would I return in a state of disgrace? I swore to myself and God that never again would I run away and leave my family in the face of danger. Even if it meant risking my life, I would stand up and fight for them. That is, if they had survived.

* * *

After a couple of hours, I came upon the hiding place where I'd left my family. There was no one there. I looked for signs of struggle: broken trees, ruffed up ground and grass, blood. There were none. Cautiously, I started for home.

As I approached my house, the squealing laughter of children reached my ears. Old Nyabwangu ran to greet me, barking happily and wagging her tail. The exhaustion from the miles I'd covered and the pain from the bruises on my feet; it all washed away with the sounds of my people. Tears of joy sprang from my eyes. I dropped to pat the old dog while they subsided.

My mother, hearing the clamor, came out of the kitchen. She greeted me with a warm mixture of surprise and relief. She busied herself fussing over my scrapes and pestering me to sit down and eat. Soon, the smell of cassava frying filled the air. I gripped a cup of warm milk.

The sweet, creamy taste assured me that I was truly home.

I looked up to see Dada walk in the door. For a moment, fear closed my throatand I almost choked. But there was nothing other than relief on his face.

"Son! I'm so glad you are safe!" he said, striding over to rub my head affectionately.

"I am sorry for disobeying your orders, father," I blurted,standing to meet him. "You're not upset with me?"

"Not at all, son," Dada said. "After you left I realized that I had made a hasty, panicked decision." He shook his head. "I exposed you to more danger. I went looking for you this morning. The fishing bay is a ghost town, hit worse than our little village. I am sorry I sent you there, and glad you were able to assess the situation and return." He looked at me with pride and love. "Now come, tell us what happened."

As I began to replay the tale of my journey through the jungle and my night with the hunter, the rest of the family trickled in the doorto listen. As soon as I'd finished, I inquired after Baaba.

"He's well, but he's worried sick about you." I could tell from the expression on Dada's face that Baaba had not approved of his decision to send me away. "Go see him, he needs to know you are back."

I found Baaba lounging where I'd left him. Before he could ask me to recant my adventures, I insisted he tell me about his encounter with the military, which my father told me came to the house while everyone was in hiding.

"I have run enough from my enemies in the past," he began with a sigh. "I will never hide from any man as long as I live. Neither tragedy nor hoodlum soldiers can break my will."

"Yes Baaba, but what did they say to you? What did they do?"

"Believe me, Rwabagabo. Nothing!" my grandfather answered with a gentle smile. He bent forward from where he sat on the hammock and took a deep breath.

I waited, looking at him anxiously. The smile on his face

grew.Slowly stretching his old legs he said, "Those foolish

soldiers asked me questions in Swahili and I answered

them in Rwandese."

A long fit of laughter shook me from my stool.

Finally, I gasped, "Why Baaba? You know they don't

understand our language!"

"Exactly, Rwabagabo. If they are going to judge me

by my heritage, then I'm proud to use my Rwandese.

Besides, it was irrelevant to discuss anything; they did

whatever they pleased. Those animals!"

"Baaba, I have to tell you--" I began, shifting my

stool to get closer so I could look him in the eye. "Your

courage is remarkable. It is a miracle they didn't shoot

you!"

"Ahh," Baaba waved my compliment away. "I

know one thing for sure: they may have guns and swords,

but I have moral authority over them. And in the end,

Rwabagabo, that is far more important."

Nine

July 1985*(Baale, Uganda)*

Wanaichi (*swahili word for citizens*)

While waiting for the rebels to return, our community was occupied by the Special Forces. We were forced to pay regular bribes of cows and money to corrupt public officials to assure protection from our own government. Despite these pay-outs, they sometimes raided villages in search of food and blood, and they maintained brutal checkpoints for those needing to travel. We kept up hope by listening to the news broadcasts, which assured us that the NRA continued to gain numbers and take territory. Thoughts of how I could aid their efforts filled my mind more and more.

One scorching Saturday, while buying food, I found

my answer. I had nearly finished the arduous task of digging a quarter sack of cassava from drought-hardened ground when the sound of people singing reached my ears. The voices became louder and clearer until finally a group came to view.

An NRA soldier led a platoon of raggedy men and women—some no older than me. Smiles broadened their young faces, and their hands clutched machetes, spears, bayonets, and hand grenades. Their jubilant leader held an AK-47. Behind the soldiers trailed a group of civilians.

In this time of war, when hopes were kept behind locked doors, the joyous public abandon of the group struck me as almost impossible. Passion and hope quickened my heartbeat. Hurriedly, I popped the final Cassavaroot out of the ground, shoved them into their burlap sack, and heaved the sack onto the bicycle. At the road, I paused to listen for the sounds of the receding rally, then took off after it.

The growing group was weaving clamorously

through the village. More people, many of them boys and girls, continued to fall in, raising their voices and farm equipment in the songs of revolution. A half-hour later, the commander stopped in the town square and ordered his men to attention.

"Hello, *wanaichi* of this land," the lieutenant greeted us.

A few shouts rang out in reply.

"As many of you know, we are the NRA," he said. "Don't worry! The Special Forces are on the run as we speak. We defeated them in Baale and we are pursuing them. That is why I stopped to communicate to you."

The audience erupted into a jubilant, "NRA *oye!*"

The lieutenant waited patiently for silence before continuing, "This is not intended to be a formal meeting; we are merely here to pass on hope and to obtain food." His gaze swept the faces of the crowd, meeting as many eyes as he could. "Unlike the ruthless government militia, we will pay for it."

"Sir, we do not want you to buy our food," a woman shouted. "We will give it to you for free! You have rescued us from the devil's grip."

"You are our heroes!" another man shouted from the back of the group.

"My son wants to join your army today!" an old man cried. "Without your army, we would be rotting in unmarked graves."

Hoots and shouts of *oye!* rang out from the crowd. Hands shot up into the air in thumbs-up gestures. The commander himself, his AK-47 slung over his back, smiled broadly and took his hat off to wave it at his still-growing audience.

I studied the calm, confident faces of the soldiers. Some were doubtless no older than me. Could I stand beside, them, gun slung over my back? Could I use that gun to kill? The answer came to me clearly. Yes. Yes, I could.

*   *   *

The rest of the day passed slowly.My mind wandered from my chores to the decision I now faced. The NRA were here, stationed near Baale. If I wanted to join them, this was my opportunity. Most of my heart rallied, full of hope and conviction, but one fresh memory seeded doubt.

Only a few days before, our civics teacher, Mr. Okot, had led my class to an overlook in Baale's surrounding foothills. "I brought you here so you would understand the consequences of war," he said. "You are the future hope of our nation; I believe that what you see today will make you better leaders of tomorrow."

Buzzing flies swarmed around us, and an acrid smell hung so strongly on the air I worried it would impregnate my skin. The smell eventually washed off; the sight that accompanied it would be with me forever.

Rotting bodies preserved in various positions of

terror littered the raw earth below. Some appeared to be crawling out of the very dirt that covered them. Our teacher explained that the victims were forced to dig their own graves. Some whom death did not find fast enough tried to escape. They did not make it far.

"The bodies below you are those of government forces and sympathizers killed by the NRA. Some were shot, others macheted by soldiers wishing to preserve their bullets," Mr.Okot explained.

His words upset me. I couldn't believe Mr.Okot could attribute this awful scene to the rebels: Gabo's men, a Tutsi-friendly army, the only hope the country had.

"Sir, how can you be sure the rebels murdered all those people?" I asked, pressing a handkerchief to my mouth even as I spoke, to prevent the stench from entering it.

"Patrick, in times of war, certainty is impossible," Mr. Okot explained. "The truth may vary depending on who you ask. Regardless, there is never justification for anyone to commit murder."

I wanted to leave, to escape the gaze of the skulls staring up at me, to run home to Baaba and Dada and demand they tell me the truth. I could not imagine getting any closer to the stench, the circling vultures, the clinging death. As we began to file silently from the grave site, a family friend walked by, head hung low, face wet with tears. She had come with her daughter to search for her husband's body. I fell in beside them to help. For an hour, we sifted through rotting bits of clothes and twisted corpses. We never found him.

That night, I could hardly eat. After dinner, I took my father aside to ask him about the graves.

"The bodies you saw were all notorious UPC leaders," he assured me. "Before they were arrested, they led the government forces into villages and caused the death of many innocent civilians! Had we not escaped into the jungle, we might have been among their victims."

"What about your friend Bulayimu? Was he really awful?" I asked, referring to the man whose body I'd searched for.

"Definitely not awful to us, but you never know when people have power. It corrupts them and they end up hurting others. There comes a time when they pay for their sins. You've heard of the Baganda saying, *'Okalyada kadada:'* 'Do wrong and there will be a price to pay'."He paused. "In my opinion, some rebel commanders rushed to kill their enemies. It was a result of a period of poor leadership. In war, these things can happen. But that does not make them a bad army. They are doing their best, and they are fighting for us."

*   *   *

As I rested with my back against an old oak tree, watching

the cows chew their cud, I kept thinking about those last words of my father. *They are fighting for us.* I should be fighting for my family as well.

Back home, I found my father carving on the veranda. Chunks of white wood lay scattered about his feet, his face set softly in thought. He looked up as I approached.

"Father," I said, meeting his gaze. "I have heard about many Tutsis in the rebel army."

"Yes, that is true," Dada replied, returning to the stick.

"Baaba doesn't like that Gabo fights for the rebels, true?" I asked.

"Not quite. Your grandfather does not like Gabo on a personal level, but he supports the rebels, and he is glad that their army is filled with Tutsi and Rwandese men. What is the meaning of all these questions, son?"

"What would you say if I joined the rebel fighters?"

Dada's eyes rose to meet mine. But before he could

answer, a thunderous voice interrupted.

"Don't think I didn't hear your outrageous question!" my mother shouted, bursting through the front door. I gulped a deep breath, "It is a reasonable question, Mama, isn't it? There are many my age in the NRA."

"No, it is not a reasonable question. You must be insane to think or utter such an idea. And you, John. I can't believe you simply looked at Patrick when he suggested it!"

"Florence," Dada said softly. "I didn't even get a chance to respond to the boy before you burst in."

"It doesn't matter," Mama declared. "There is no more to say. This conversation should never be brought up again."

My mother stormed back into the house, slamming the door.

*   *   *

That night, I could not sleep. The rebel commander's propaganda swirled in my head like a cyclone, competing with my mother's impassioned worries. Images of her anger and tears arose, but in my heart I knew I needed to do what was right for my family—even if that meant disobeying Mama. A plan coalesced in my mind, bringing with it a measure of peace. Finally, sleep snatched me away to a thought-free world.

Afande (senior *soldier)*

The rooster had not yet begun his morning song when I woke with a surge of adrenaline. In the faint pre-dawn glow, I slipped out of bed and tiptoed to the door, grabbing only a few slices of cassava, my plastic shoes, and the small brown leather wallet Baaba had given me on my last graduation. Just outside I heard sniffs and snorts: my dog,

Simba, waiting for me. Inside there were only the soft snores of my siblings.

I hesitated, my hand trembling inches from the handle of our squeaky door. Dada hadears like a watchdog. Any motion made, whether inside or outside, he heard. There was no way I could get out without waking him. Better to be preemptive.

"Dada . . . Dada are you awake?" I called softly, pressing my nose to the crack of my parent's door.

There was a rustling. Then, a tired voice: "Yes, what do you need?"

"I need to go to school early today."

"School? On the weekend?"

"Yes, we have a soccer tournament coming up soon and our coach wants us to train."

"I thought you weren't interested in soccer!"My heart skipped two beats, but as I struggled to respond, he continued, "Okay, can you help with milking first?"

"No, Dada, the coach was adamant that we must be there before seven."

"Okay then, we will see you when you return."

I sent up a brief prayer of thanks and turned to leave. As I reached the doorway, another voice froze me in place.

"Patrick, would you like to borrow your father's bicycle?"

"No, mama, I will ride with a friend who is coming to meet on the way," I answered.

"Remember to eat something before you go," she murmured, her voice trailing off back into sleep.

"I already did, thank you. Have a nice day!"

With the door finally closed behind me, I let out a tense lungful of air. The sky took on a faint glow. A gentle breeze turned the dried grasses into whispering instruments. I took a last look at our sleeping herd of cattle, the thatched huts, the old mulberry tree with its stained ground and sturdy trunk that my father and I loved. As my gaze traveled the blue shadows of my home, my hesitation fell away. Without doubt, I would fight to the death for this heritage, this home, and the family that lay sleeping behind that thin door. With Simba at my heels, I took off running down the dirt path to Baale.

*   *   *

By the time I arrived, dawn had found the town, and sounds of life were beginning to trickle from open windows. As I jogged along the main street, the foothills loomed at the edges of my vision. I could no longer think of them without seeing the mass graves hiding in their crevices. Faint waves of nausea, and a fear of both killing and being killed, rose in me. I tried to push the thoughts from my mind.

The rebels were stationed about a kilometer from town. As I neared the base, a young soldier zoomed past, revving his Kawasaki motorcycle's engine to full speed. Seeing me, he slammed on his rear brakes, skidding in a 180-degree turn that filled the air with dust and exhaust. He revved his engine gleefully as he putted back towards me. I could tell from his slim face, long nose and slender physique that he was Tutsi like me. He put out a friendly hand.

"*Nibite, shaa?*"

"*Nibyiza. Nibite byawe?*" I greeted him back, smiling at the energy with which he shook my hand. His was sweaty and vibrating from the motorcycle ride, mine from nervousness and the exertion of running.

"Where are you going?". His hand returned to play with the throttle.

"I … I want to join you."

"Join me?" he asked. A brown-toothed smile spread over his face. "You mean join us, the NRA!"

"Yes."

"Very exciting!" His words came tumbling on top of each other. "You will realize freedom and power. Go on towards that gate, the men there will help you. I am with the reconnaissance and special mission detachment. I hope to see you when you finish training." He sped off, leaving behind a plume of red dust.

Two soldiers stood guard at a makeshift wooden gate at the entrance to the rebel compound. Though no fence surrounded the camp, the villagers knew and respected its boundaries.

The soldiers were tall, fit, and heavily armed. Hand grenades and pistols weighted their belts. One sported an AK-47 slung casually over his shoulder while the other leaned against a fence post. As I approached, Simba hurried up beside me, his hackles bristling. I orderedhim to stay behind.

"Good morning sir," I greeted the soldiers. The one who had been leaning on his bayonet-fitted gun straightened and approached me with wary red-rimmed eyes.

"What do you want?" He asked. His teeth worked a wad of chewing gum as though he were angry at it.

"Sir, I would like to join the NRA," I replied, trying to sound humble and confident all at once.

"What? Are you a spy?"

"No, sir. I'm just a civilian interested in being part of your good army."

"Who told you we are recruiting?"

"No one, sir," I answered. Behind me, Simba resumed his growling. My uneasiness grew.

"Wait here," he ordered, and disappeared into an aluminum building. His colleague sat by the gate, pulling smoke from his cigarette and acting as if I did not exist.

Doubt crept in. The attitudes of these soldiers put me off— so different from those I had met in the village, or even the motorcycle-loving soldier I'd just met on the road.

War, I reminded myself, is complicated.

The ill-tempered guard returned, followed by a fully uniformed soldier with a pip on his shirt indicating he was a second lieutenant.

"I am Afande Kiwenda," the soldier said, stretching out his callused hand. His firmhandshake made me think of a politician.

"Glad to meet you, sir. I'm Patrick."

"Get rid of your stupid dog and come with me," Afande Kiwenda ordered.

"Simba is not stupid, sir. He's a good friend," I replied.

The lieutenant gave me a piercing scowl. "Get your mangy dog out of here."

Tamping down the surge of anger and fear that tightened my throat, I stepped back to where I'd told my loyal dog to wait. Behind me I heard the soldiers laughing. That didn't bother me as much as their insult to Simba.

I knelt down to look my dog in the eyes. He tilted his head sideways and eyed me as if asking that I reconsider my plan. "No, Simba, this is it!" I told him, speaking softly so the soldiers wouldn't hear. "I have become a man and I must do what is right for myself and all Rwandese people."

Simba didn't seem so sure of all this, but he raised and stood up. When I waved him on, he trotted away with his tail hung low between his legs, pausing once to throw me a final mournful look. Since he was a six-month-old puppy, Simba had followed me everywhere, including to school in Baale town. I knew he'd find his way home.

With Simba gone, I followed Afande Kiwenda towards the shoddy offices. The place seemed deserted and run down. There were two aluminum storage sheds, one of which echoed with a sound that reminded me of dying bats. The other's door swung open brokenly, and I could see that it was empty. The smell of rat feces and cigarette smoke gave the air a sour twist. We passed a couple of other soldiers, lounging quietly, jaws working on gum or cigarettes, eyes far off, before entering the shack that contained the officer's wobbly old desk. A dirty cup of porridge canted on top of a manila folder and its spilled contents. Hanging on the officer's chair were an AK-47 and a transceiver radio that crackled with sound.

"Training starts now," Afande Kiwenda announced, sitting rigidly down behind the desk and pushing the folder out of the way. The chair wobbled in disagreement. He cleared his throat.

"First, you refer to any soldier with a higher rank than yours by the title 'Sir' or 'Lieutenant.' Second, you do not ask questions without permission. Third, you do not do anything, including taking a piss, without permission. Fourth, always be ready for anything. And fifth, Afande is always right! Understood?"

"Yes, sir," I agreed.

"And your response should always be "sir, yes sir' spoken loudly and with your chin up," Afande corrected, demonstrating proper chin posture.

I met what I took to be a welcoming joke with a smile, but he remained stoic and serious. My smile waned. I raised my chin and replied, "Sir, yes sir."

"Why do you want to join the NRA?" he asked.

"I would like to fight the government military before they come back and kill me and my family."

"Precisely!" Afande Kiwenda said, rapping his desk with a strong fist. "Although there is more to this cause than your personal reasons, I sense that you are determined to be a liberator. You notice I didn't use the word fighter, but liberator. This is a struggle to liberate our country and people like the Tutsis who are suffering under the Uganda People's Congress, the UPC regime." He gave me a long, sharp look., and then added, "I know enough of you already. You will have plenty of teaching and training later.

In the meantime, wait until we get more recruits. Then a convoy to take you down to the barracks."

"Sir, yes, sir," I answered.

Without ceremony, the afandeleft me with stern orders not to leave my chair without asking permission. While I waited to be transferred, I watched the yard through the metal hut's pane-less window. In a far corner, one combatant punished another by forcing him to rub his own face in the mud. The songbirds twittered above, oblivious. Occasional curses and shouts broke the calm.

Suddenly, a camouflaged Land Rover full of soldiers drove through the open gate. It screeched to a stop just a few feet from the office where I sat.

Singing in jubilation, a band of soldiers jumped off the cruiser. They waved their guns in the air, stomped their feet to salute their seniors, and gestured proudly to their catch—two captives, stripped to their underwear, their hands cuffed tightly behind their backs. The captive'sbodies glowed with sweat, and they stumbled weakly as the still-singing soldiers pushed them out of the truck and led them out of sight. Images of the mass graves behind Baale flashed through my head.

*   *   *

The sun was beginning its descent when a stone-faced soldier finally ordered me into the same stripped-down Land Cruiser. Five heavily-armed rebels clamored in beside me, along with another recruit around my age.

We sped off towards the barracks, the truck swaying and bouncing off the rutted earth. The soldiers, most of them in their teens, didn't seem affected by the wild ride. "Go pilot! Fly like a fighter MIG plane," one shouted at the top of his voice. "*Twende*!" cried the others, "let's go!" Occasionally, the other recruit and I exchanged tight smiles, to show that we weren't bothered by the reckless driving, but I could see that his hands clutched the sides of the truck as tightly as mine.

Forty-five minutes later, we arrived at the barracks. Dense forest surrounded a scattering of grass-thatched huts. After the disarray of the intake office and the rattling roar of the ride there, the quiet order of the place filled me with relief. Men walked about purposefully, some with rifles slung over their shoulders, some carrying firewood or sacks of food. A few lay the thatching for a new hut, while in a distance the others marched in formation. Two of the soldiers jumped down from the truck to escort the other recruit and I into a centrally located grass-thatched building.

An officer with a heavy moustache and night-black skin sat behind a two-way radio.He smelled of stale cigarettes. Eyes fixed on the large black box, he barked commands in Swahili. A soldier stood next to him taking notes.

"Lieutenant Siade," one of the young soldiers said to announce our presence, saluting the commander.

The officer's eyes still didn't move from the radio. He put his hand out to signal silence and listened intently to a stretch of crackly noise.

We waited behind the desk for several minutes. Abruptly, the commander flipped off the radio and jerked his attention towards us. He raised his hand to the black beret obscuring his forehead, made a brief salute, and asked, "Are those *kurutus*?"

"Sir, yes, sir," the soldier answered, confirming that we were the new recruits.

"Hey kurutus, come closer. Quickly!" the afande ordered. He dismissed the soldiers who brought us.

"I know why you are here," he said. "It had better not be for anyreason other than to defend and liberate this country from tyranny. Anything else on your mind, we will find out and kill you faster than you can say your mothers' names! You hear me?" The senior officer shot us a harsh glance, placedhis palms on the desk and stood swiftly.

I flinched, though the other boy remained steady.

"There is a soldier waiting outside to direct you to food and a place to sleep," he said. "Training starts tomorrow. Now go!"

*   *   *

The next morning, the call to order came just before five. While I was accustomed to such early hours, many of the new recruits were not. Others were still rubbing their eyes and making their way reluctantly out of the tent where we'd slept while I already stood in formation with a clean face and brushed teeth. The cool of night still clung, and a steady drizzle darkened our clothes.

A soldier built like a bulldog strolled our straggly line.

"I am Sergeant Singa! Are you ready?"

We were too scared to answer.

"You new recruits need to learn respect! Now, let me hear you answer."

"Sir, yes, sir," we replied.

"Lesson number one," the sergeant said. "I ask and you answer! You answer right away, too. Is that clear, kurutus?"

"Sir, yes, sir," we all answered in unison and clearly.

"Good start, but I need more enthusiasm. I need to hear a strong, fierce voice that can disarm an enemy!" The trainer continued to pace before us, kicking one young recruit's boots into line and lifting another's chin. He paused before me, took a scornful look at my shoes and said, "You think those cheap plastic shoes will be sufficient for your training?"

"I don't..." I began, but he was already down the

line, heckling another kurutu.

Lieutenant Siade hurried in from across the compound. After saluting Sergeant Singa, he inspected our line, a sour look on his face. Silence hung, knotting my empty stomach.

Finally, he spoke. "This is the beginning of your training. Some of you are shaking because of the little rain this morning. Let me tell you that rain never stops the NRA. Even Mzee Museveni, our commander, would be standing here if he needed to."

For two hours, Afande Siade carried on about the strength and integrity of the rebel fighters, the heart of the NRA cause, and our roles in this historical movement. He spoke in Swahili, which I learned would be our primary language of communication. His lectures emphasized obedience, discretion, and respect, but above all a total dedication to our leader, Mzee Museveni.

Finally, he left us with a salute and the command to

stand at ease. Afande Singa returned to take over our training.

We spent the rest of the day practicing formations and performing various chores around the base. The familiarity of collecting water and firewood eased my nervousness a little. Long after nightfall, we ate a simple but filling meal by the faint light of kerosene lanterns and a crescent moon. Afterwards, all the kurutus and officers assembled around a huge bonfire for our evening briefing. With the meeting over, we were finally able to relax. Conversations, story-telling, and singing filled the night. The raging fire and the camaraderie I found around it burned off the doubts instilled earlier that day by my rude introduction into the NRA army.

*   *   *

For the next couple of weeks, we trained and worked from

sun up to sun down. Lieutenant Said led us in strengthening drills and chores, as well as in building *manyata*, the "huts" that became our homes. Afande Siade and another ranking officer instructed us in combat. We learned to escape enemy ambush, to take cover during fire, and how to handle torture and interrogation. They armed us with AK-47s and swords, instructing us in charges, direct combat, and how to support each other and the elite platoons during combat. Lieutenant Siade infused our minds with the doctrine of the rebel cause, and soon my heart thumped and my sweat poured with the sole purpose of serving both the NRA and Museveni. I was no longer afraid of fighting—I was beginning to itch for it.

"This army prepares you to win battles," Afande Siade said, pacing our platoon after target practice. He no longer looked at us sourly, but with a mutual pride that strengthened the bond of leader to troops. I stood proudly holding my AK-47. "We are a professional army and we will never put you in combat irresponsibly. You will see; your first experience will be one you'll never forget. There is nothing like it. And you will come back a respected soldier whom everybody will admire. The NRA will raise your status and the villages will chant praises in your name. You will be a hero!

"Are you ready to fight and die for your country and for your people?"

Our guns thumped the ground in unison.

"Yes, Afande, yes!"

My voice rose above the others, strong and clear.

Ten

August 1985 *(Baale, Uganda)*

Kadogo *(little one)*

An eerie emptiness at the barracks marked the day of my first armed mission. No one called us to order that morning.Unsure of how to proceed, my comrades and I went about our duties like usual. Save for the occasional exchange of firm-mouthed looks, we didn't mention the lack of command, not even to oneanother.

After breakfast we went to the area where drills were usually held, but there was no officer present. We waited for half an hour in the strangely still camp. Finally, an announcement echoed through the rustle of the surrounding jungle: we were to assemble in front of Lieutenant Siade's office.

"Maybe one of our commanders was ambushed and

killed by the enemy last night," I muttered to Lumala, a young soldier who shared my *manyata,* as we marched double time to the office.

"I doubt that, but I have a feeling we are about to hear something bad," he replied.

Sergeant Singa was there when we arrived. Wrinkles cut deep furrows in his forehead as he called us to order.

Calm fell quickly upon the assembled soldiers. Even the trees seemed to still as Lieutenant Siade appeared before us, inspecting our formation with a critical eye. He slapped the flat side of the bayonet in his palm, and the sound echoed down the line.

"We have intel about a planned ambush by the government army," he began. The hairs on the back of my neck prickled with anticipation of his next words. "We are going to preempt their mission by attacking first. Every single one of you will have a role in supporting our elite platoon. Whatever Sergeant Singa and I tell you, take it serious. If you miss anything, you will be killed or get someone else killed. And remember this: soldiers who are captured by the enemy experience worse torment than those who are shot."

With a nod, the Afande left us in heavy silence. We shifted uneasily as we waited for our departure. As time crawled by, my courage evaporated like dew on a leaf hit by the morning sun. I began a silent prayer for a change in the day's plan.

My heart jumped when I heard the rattle of three trucks coming down to our barracks. There was no time to dwell on reservations. As the lorries parked, Sergeant Singa instructed my platoon to follow him to the weapons closet. Being the newest and lowest ranking of the soldiers, we had not yet been issued our own. We'd fight with whatever aged and hopefully sharp-edged equipment we were handed. The sergeant passed out pangas, spears, and bayonets. A few of the soldiers with more advanced training received worn shotguns. I got a bayonet. It bore only a faint twinkle of orange rust, and the edge sparkled menacingly in the sun.

Clutching my weapon with as casual an ease as I could fake, I clamored into one of the trucks with the rest of my platoon. We tried to sit cool and calm, our faces masks of sweating stone. The three senior officers in our lorry appeared lost in deep thought, and all was silent save the rumbling engines of the trucks.

After a half-hour, we rolled through a quiet village. There were no people, just a few chickens and goats moving slowly across the beaten ground. The trucks pulled to a halt, and we jumped out and stood at attention. Three other platoons lined up beside us.

A transformed Lieutenant Siade paced our ranks. A black beret topped his head at a haughty angle, and a jacket of bullet magazines cut across his green camouflage shirt.

He wore grenades across his chest and a large black pistol on his hip. His AK-47 had a razor-sharp bayonet. The stern cool rage on his features both chilled and reassured me-- this was a man whose experience and knowledge of combat could be relied upon. He was the kind of leader a soldier wants to follow into battle.

"Soldiers," Lieutenant Siade addressed us. His voice came out as smooth and deadly as his attire. "You are here to defend your country from the ruthless government killers. I know you are well trained for the task ahead. Let's go show them fire power!"

"Sir, yes, sir!" we replied and stamped our feet in salute.

Lieutenant Siade and the other afandes led our platoons a mile into the forest, through thorny bushes and across rushing creeks. I barely felt the chill of water or the strain of our quick pace. When the lieutenant called us to a halt, adrenaline trickled through my veins like acid.

"In a few minutes, our elite platoon will attack the government military detachment in Kitwe, right beyond that hill," he rumbled, gesturing ahead. "Immediately after the attack, your duty is to disarm the surrendered soldiers, empty their armory, and help our injured where necessary. Be wary of the enemy. Some play dead and they will kill you. If you sense any breath, finish him off. If you confiscate a gun, don't hesitate to use it."

Five, ten minutes ticked by, and then we heard gunfire erupting.

"*Vumiria,* 'stay still,' " the afande ordered as a few of the boys around me jerked or ducked instinctively from the booming explosions. The acrid odor of panic mixed with that of mud and rotting vegetation. Tears and sweat shone on the faces of my fellow kurutus, their eyes wide and white. Rocket-propelled grenades roared through the empty sky above like fire-breathing dragons. In the cacophony, my mind achieved stillness: I was ready for a fight.

As the shelling began to peter out, Afande Siade ordered us to advance.

Feet rustling, heads low, we moved up and over a hill, the town opening up before us. The government quarters were the first structures we reached. One of our men was hunched against the wall of the nearest building as if he wished to melt into it. He clutched his belly with a blood-sticky hand, but nodded us on as we fanned out to search the area. The troops we were there to support sprinted, their comrades covering them with gunfire. Bodies of enemy soldiers littered the ground in awkward khaki heaps.

Our platoon of kurutus followed in the wake of the advancing soldiers. We moved between the fallen bodies, first checking to make sure they were dead, then patting them down for guns and other valuables. The smell of sulfur intensified as we moved to the center of the government stronghold. It would forever after fill my mouth with the metallic taste of war.

Afande Singa ordered me to break out from the group and head east towards where a group of houses clustered, their walls and ceilings ripped to their frames. Their interior lay cracked and exposed, walls were blasted away to frame what they had once sheltered. My heart beat a steady, throbbing lump in my throat as I moved into the crumbling shadows of destruction. The sounds around me became dull and muffled. I'd never felt so alone, nor so exposed. I kept my back tight to the wall as I turned into an alley between the buildings.

A dark face with war-frenzied eyes jerked up to meet mine. I froze briefly, my hands tightening on my bayonet, and a wave of invincible power and terror surged though to my finger tips. For a split second I knew I could kill. Then, I took in the uniform of a fellow NRA soldier, and a rush of air left my lungs. The scrawny boy looked only a few years older than me, and he clutched his gun in a death grip. I could see the faintest tremble from his trigger hand. Three enemy soldiers knelt before him, hands on their heads, facing away.

"Quick, go back and get any afande you can find," the boy ordered, quickly returning his eyes to the captives.

I ran back towards where I'd left Afande Singa. I found him directing a few of the other boys from my platoon. "Sir," I told him, rushing a salute. "We've captured three enemy soldiers."

I raced back towards the captives with the afande on my heels. He sprinted ahead of me when we rounded the corner, hurtling himself in front of the captives. Without hesitation, he issued a series of rib-cracking kicks to their stomachs. "*Lala chin*, 'lie down'." He spat.

The men dropped to the earth in a groaning wave.

"*Kadogo*, 'little one,'" Sergeant Singa commanded the young soldier. "Search them. Should they move, slice their heads off."

"With your permission, afande," the teenage rebel asked, "Can I just shoot them instead?"

"No! We need to save our bullets," Afande Singa ordered.

"Kadogo, Patrick, remove everything except for their underwear."

Our captives panted like dogs fresh from the hunt as I stripped them. Afterward, the afande had cuffed them so tightly that I thought their shoulders would dislocate and their skin would rip. At first, I felt guilty to be treating them so disrespectfully, and with far less care than we'd show a cow during castration. Then, one of the soldier's eyes met mine. They were full of blind hate. I no longer saw a fellow man but a rapist, a killer, one of the soldiers who had driven my family from our home and into hiding and who threatened to drive my people out of yet another country. My anger returned.

Afande Singa instructed the other young soldier to load the captives onto our trucks. With the waning of battle, they had roared into the town's armory to collect the troops. "Don't let your eyes leave them for a moment, not even to blink. If they escape, we will shoot you as well," he warned.

With a parting nod to my fellow soldier, I followed the afande to the armory. There, I joined the rest of my platoon in collecting weapons, medicine, cigarettes, shoes, and clothing while the victory songs of our soldiers began to trickle in through the blasted walls, filling the air with vibrant energy. Even the occasional shot that rang out had a triumphant pitch to it.

As we rolled through the town of Baale with our spoils and captives, people cheered us until tears made their faces glisten, and sang us songs of praise until their voices were hoarse. They skipped alongside the swaying open-back trucks, where I sat proudly, clutching my bayonet at my side. A feeling of importance and meaning swelled my chest. In the town square, Lieutenant Siade preached NRA propaganda to the joyous villagers as I stood straight-spined and stone-faced beside my fellow soldiers.

"These killers you see," the afande said, pointing his gun to the three captives, "Are cowards in uniform. Come join us so such men will not rule over you."

The crowd applauded. On the faces of the young men and their fathers, I read a familiar desire.

*　　　*　　　*

Back at the barracks, the celebration continued. We built a raging bonfire, and as night fell we sang and danced with ever-increasing jubilation. The commanders clinked bottles of beer, and so many cigarettes were passed that their smoke thickened the air. Finally, a smiling Lieutenant

Siade called us to order.

"Today was a victory," Saide said. "We had a few casualties, but no deaths on our side. This is something to celebrate, but do not believe that it is the usual. For some of you new soldiers, this is just the beginning. You will experience far more blood on the battlefield, and some of it may be yours. We have a long war ahead."

*   *   *

As usual the call to order came before sunrise the next morning, but for the first time since I'd arrived at the barracks, I was not on a five-minute count-down to get ready and put my toes on a line. That was for the new recruits, and I was no longer a *kurutu.*

"I am so glad we don't have to cut trees and make huts anymore," I mused to a fellow soldier over breakfast.

"Every dog has its day," he replied. "I'm hatching a

nasty practical joke for *kurutus*," he added with a wink.

"C'mon, man," I said. "We don't have to treat them as badly as we were treated."

"It happened to us, it's got to happen to them," he said with a shrug, pushing himself up from the long makeshift wooden table and grabbing his dishes. "Let's go to the formation before Lieutenant Siade does."

*   *   *

Lieutenant Siade pulled dark sunglasses from his face and fixed us with a steadfast gaze. "You have experienced war. You know what it means to conquer your enemy, defend the civilians of this country, and make our leader Museveni proud! You are soldiers of the National Resistance Army-- advanced training begins today!"

His gaze went down the line, passing over each of us. "You will now carry guns at all times," he commanded.

At a weapons shed, we received our regulation AK-47s in solemn excitement. The gun was nearly as large as my torso, sleek metal and dark wood. As the lieutenant led us on a mile-long march towards the advanced training area, I felt very conscious of the strap across my chest, the shifting weight on my back. I felt powerful.

Afande Singa called us to attention in an open field, hedged in by a swamp on one side and forest on the other. We fell immediately into formation, saluting as one.

"These combat drills will be intense," he barked, spit flying from his sun-cracked lips. "They are war drills. You must follow commands carefully to avoid accidents."

He stepped forward and his arm swept a grand arc. "Make a line, side by side, stretching the entire field. Turn right. Then turn right again!"

The order left us facing the open field, with our backs to the senior officers.

In a thunderous voice Lieutenant Siade

commanded, "Ready? Advance!"

We all moved forward hesitantly, unsure of what to expect, or exactly what was expected of us. Without warning, one of the afandes fired a bullet overhead. We dove to the ground.

"Good, now crawl forward!" Lieutenant Siade called out.

With our guns held in front of us, we slithered across the wet grass, our bodies thrashing like crocodiles.

"Roll over! Take cover! Advance! Roll! Crawl!" Siade barked ruthlessly, each new order piling on top of the last before it was even completed. "Now get up and run!"

Glad to be off the ground, I took off sprinting. Years of running with our herd through the bushes and pastures had prepared me for this part well; my long lean muscles carried me and two other boys ahead of the others. The gun moved roughly against my back but didn't hinder my stride.

"Take cover," the lieutenant ordered, and with a smooth leap, I dove into the brush on the edge of the swap. All but two other boys were far behind, still out in the grassy field. "Advance!" the lieutenant ordered. I hesitated at the edge of the black sticky vegetation, casting my eyes over towards the other soldiers.

"What are you fools waiting for?" Lieutenant Siade barked. "It's a bullet from the enemy or a shitty marsh! You choose." He fired into the air, sending us sprinting into the mire.

An RPG soared overhead, taking down a huge Acacia on a hill a field away. "Run to that tree and show it no mercy with your bayonets! I want to see it chipped to dirt!" Siade instructed, pointing to the smoking stump.

I emerged from the swamp neck and neck with two other soldiers. The thrill of competition fueled the surging adrenaline from the explosives flying overhead, the lieutenant's rapid orders, the heavy presence of a high-powered weapon on my back. I was so focused on reaching the stump ahead of the others that I barely saw the grass that fell away beneath my feet. Suddenly, something pulled me down into a crumpled heap.

Pain radiated up my body in hot waves. At first, I was sure a landmine had gotten me--I wondered if the shock had been so great it had deafened me to the noise. Then, I looked down to see my right leg disappearing into the huge metal the jaws of an animal trap. Blood seeped out around its crushing prongs. Grabbing helplessly at my knee, I threw back my head in a deep, animal howl.

In a few seconds, Lieutenant Siade was at my side, bending down to examine my injury. "*Kadogo!*" he said. "Don't move; just wait." He pulled the trap off my leg, his eyes squinting red with the effort. Blood gushed from the gaping holes the metal teeth left, soaking my leg, and bringing with it another wave of impossible pain. I let out another throat-ripping scream.

"You!" the lieutenant ordered, nodding to one of the two boys who'd been racing beside me. The other soldiers had begun to gather around us in a loose circle. "Rip your t-shirt into a bandage and hand it to me."

He rolled the t-shirt and wrapped it around my ankle, then instructed two soldiers to lift me up. I watched, faintly mesmerized, as blood bloomed through the makeshift tourniquet.

"I'm sorry, friend," the Lieutenant said to me, wiping my blood off his hands and onto his cargo pants. The gentle care in his voice surprised me.

"Afande, am I going to lose my leg?" I asked. Doubt had begun to trickle into my pain-numbed mind: fear that my future in the army was in jeopardy. I knew there was no place on the battlefield for a one-legged soldier.

"Don't talk like that," he advised. "Brave soldiers never quit." He picked up my gun and raised his fist in a gesture of courage and solidarity. "Now let's get you to the clinic. The bandage was already soaked through."

Dwaliro *(a clinic)*

The NRA's medical clinic occupied the corner of a one-story cinderblock warehouse two kilometers away over heavily rutted roads. A soldier took me there as carefully as he could on the back of his motorcycle, but each bump sent a red seismic wave from my ankle to my head. The pain ricocheted through my body, leaving room for nothing else.

In the *dwaliro*, the clinic, the soldier lay me out on a low cot. A stern-faced woman came over, dressed in a faded and stained smock. Her kinky hair escaped raggedly from its knot atop her head. She removed my makeshift bandage, examined my injury, and gave me an injection of pain medication.

"This is going to need stitches," she said as she disinfected the wound and wrapped it tightly in white gauze. "You'll also need a tetanus vaccine, which we don't have here. I'm afraid your injuries are beyond the scope of what we're set up to handle."

When I tried to respond, bile rose in my throat, so I simply lay quietly and waited for the pain medicine to set in. I felt lightheaded, my thoughts vague and unfocused like the red glow of the world that came in through my closed eyelids.

"Do you live near here?" the nurse was asking.

"Yes, only four hours walking distance." The words swam from my mouth, without my permission, tasting of blood. "Why?" Around me the world twisted in near-focus, empty grey walls.

"Young man, this injury is going to keep you in bed for a while. I have to talk to your commander and see what he wants to do with you."

"Do with me?" A rush of panic dispersed the fog in my brain. I lifted my head from the pillow and my eyes latched onto hers.

The woman stared back at me, her foreheadwrinkled.She pulling off her red-stained plastic gloves. Behind her, the empty makeshift clinic made no promises. A few dirty metal bowls canted in the corner. Stained rags hung over a metal bed frame.

"Don't tell them to let me go, please."

She shook her head, pulled up the bed sheet to cover me, and walked away.

I'd ceased to imagine a future for myself outside of the army. Even though it had been only four weeks in camp, being a soldier and fighting for my people and my family were the right course. In the numb confusion of themedication, my thoughts swam with the possibility of going back to being a farmer, a student, a son.

The nurse returned with an old plastic mug and a fist full of tablets. "Here, take these," she commanded. "They will help prevent infection."

I hated taking tablets, and my throat felt dry as cotton. I wasn't sure I could even swallow them. I asked, "Can I get another injection instead?"

"Take the medicine or you will risk losing that leg," she answered curtly. Her outstretched fist hung above me.

I sighed. Even with the cup of water she offered, the pills cut my throat like razors. "What is going to happen to me?" I asked once I'd choked them down.

"Just relax and try to get some sleep. The commander will tell you your fate in the morning."

Before she left, she extinguished the kerosene lantern. I was the only patient in the sick bay that evening, and with the darkness came deep silence. Soon, the narcotics stilled my pain and my burning mind as sleep overtook me.

*   *   *

I woke to a throbbing pain in my right ankle. My first wish was to return to sleep, but Lieutenant Siade stood by my bed, calling my name.

"Hello, *Kadogo* Patrick, how are you feeling?"

"Not so good, the pain is back," I answered. "Where is the nurse?"

"She will be here shortly," Siade said. "But listen, I want to talk to you about a critical decision we've made." He sat down on the edge of my bed, turning his long legs so they would fit between the closely spaced cots.

"We are going to send you home today. Your injury is serious; it could cripple you if you don't receive adequate care. Unfortunately, we have no doctors of our own in this area. We cannot bring you to a hospital capable of treating you; it is too dangerous for us to be seen in such public places. Your family must care for you at this point."

"Sir, I will be ready to go back into combat in just a few days," I croaked, struggling to lift myself up. The

297

movement sent pain rushing through me, and I stifled a moan and sank back into the bed.

The afande looked at me sympathetically. "You will understand later that this was the right decision."

"But sir, I am a good soldier. I can still fight."

"For now, just concentrate on getting better."

Afande Siade got up and started to walk away. Before he exited, he turned around and said, "By the way, your mother came to the base looking for you earlier this month, but due to military rules, we couldn't allow you a visitor. She will be happy to see you."

He looked me up and down and gave a nod. "Make sure you return here as soon as you heal. This," he gestured at my leg, "was an unfortunate accident. But you have what it takes to become a great soldier, and be of benefit to this army, to your country. This will not stop you."

"Thank you, sir!" I breathed. Those last words, and the hope that they carried, were better balm than any pain medication.

*   *   *

Sergeant Singa had me home by two o'clock that afternoon. The injury, the pain, everything seemed a blur as we rolled slowly into the landscape of my home. It was all unchanged but somehow turned unfamiliar by my own transformation. I felt as though I'd been gone years instead of weeks. Mama sat outside on a leather mat in front of the kitchen, looking as if she'd been waiting there since I'd left against her will. From the expression on her face, I could not tell if she was angry or happy. But when I stepped off the motorcycle, balancing carefully on my good leg, she pulled me into a long embrace.

"Thank God you are home!" she said. The words came out tight and slow, as if she were keeping them from exploding from her chest. "You are a fighter, Patrick. I feared this would happen. I'm thankful to God you made it home alive."

"I'm sorry, Mama," I managed. I didn't know what more to say.

My father appeared from the *kraal*. He greeted me with usual gruffness, but as the sergeant took him aside for a brief chat, he squinted as if to hide his shining eyes.

"Look how thin and dark you've become!" Mama said as she finally released me. "Let's get you inside.

I saluted Sergeant Singa and let Mama bear most of my weight as I hobbled into the house. My sisters, who had been peering out the door, now gathered around, the younger ones looking at me with wide eyes while the elders dotingly tended to me.

Robinah tucked a pillow under my head, while Joyce appeared with a glass of fresh, warm milk. It soothed my sore throat, and with the familiar flavor and smell came my first real feeling of being home. Simba wandered in the open door and lay next to me, wagging his tail and happily licking my hand.

I sipped my milk, burying my fingers in Simba's fur. Outside, I heard Sergeant Singa's motorcycle rumble away. One by one, more people filtered into the house. Mama put a steaming plate of fried beans on my stomach.

There was a brief pause, and then a barrage of questions from my siblings.

"So, did you shoot people?" Annet asked, her voice louder than the others.

"Annet, please!" Robinah yelled.

Just then, Baaba came in through the open door. The room fell silent. He moved slowly and carefully, his skin hanging in loose wrinkles from his face, his once-tall frame more hunched and shrunken than ever. It seemed as though he'd aged two years in two months.

"Oh, Rwabagabo," Baaba said, taking my hand warmly in both of his as he gazed down at me with watery eyes. "I'm so glad you are alive."

"As we all are," Mama said, sitting down next to me. She wiped quickly at her eyes and straightened her spine. "But, I think now is a good time for you to tell us why you abandoned your family and betrayed our trust."

"Florence," Baaba said, still holding my hand and gazing at me gently. "Take it easy on my grandson."

"Mama," I said, "My leg hurts so much, I beg a little rest."

"Well, you're not going to be able to AVOID ME forever, boy," she vowed. "I'm not done with you."

Later that night, as I lay in bed listening to the strange calm of home, I heard Mama and Dada talking out in the living room.

"As far as I'm concerned, he will never return to the army," my mother vowed.

"The situation is not all that bad, Florence," Dada argued. "What happened was an accident. And the sergeant who dropped him off said that Patrick holds great potential as a soldier, that he's fearless on the battlefield. "

"What kind of army allows children to fight?" she demanded.

"Patrick isn't a child any more, Florence. And the soldier who dropped him off had a good explanation for this situation, if you would listen."

"There is no explanation for any of this," Mama said, her voice full of fury. "If you allow him to return to the army, the next time they will drop off a carcass."

Eleven

January, 1986 (Baale, Uganda)

I lived a very different life after returning home. My military training made me untouchable by bullies and I was showered with attention. My ankle healed quickly due to the good doctors at Kayunga Hospital, though the costs of the treatment took a little longer to recover from--Baaba dug into his savings, father sold two cows and borrowed money from friends, and the whole family had to ration food for a month.

I'd been home about three months when the NRA officially overthrew the Uganda National Liberation Frontand assumed government of Uganda. The date was

January 26, 1986, and I remember it well because I spent hours that night waiting in Galiraya at the distillery to pick up my father's *waragi* order. A hush fell over the trading center as the announcement came over the many crackling transistor radios perched and hung in various open-front shops lining the street. A tidal wave of joyous relief followed the din. Singing and dancing erupted in the streets and bottles of *waragi* were passed between friends. I loaded my order and pedaled furiously through the jungle to celebrate the news with my family. Dada's supply of alcohol went quickly, and no one went to bed until the sun had cracked the horizon.

*   *   *

Two weeks later, on a drizzly morning, I asked Dada if I could borrow his bicycle to ride to school.

"What for?" he asked from where he lounged under

the mulberry tree. His eyes and voice seemed scratchy and tired. "Your injury is long-past healed."

"We are taking examinations today," I said, "and I would like to get there early."

"Well, you could have started walking sooner, but . . ." He waved a dismissive hand, "it might rain. Take your sisters, too," he added.

With Joyce shifting uncomfortably on the frame and Robinah on the carrier, I pedaled off into the gray morning. Midway between home and school, there was a community waterstationalongside the road. There were no villagers there this morning, working the hand-pump to fill their containers; only a lone man in a long, green, military-style jacket. Immediately, my senses keened--he was a stranger, and he did not look friendly.

"Look at that man. He looks troubled or insane," Joyce noted.

"No, he's just shabby!" Robinah argued.

I shushed them as we drew into earshot. The stranger's red eyes fixated on us as we approached. He stepped in front of the bicycle, forcing me to swerve to a stop. The girls clung tenuously to the frame.

"Where are you going?" the man demanded. Debris matted his overgrown hair, as though he had slept in the bushes. His dark complexion magnified a gaunt, frowning face. I couldn't tell whether he was angry or simply ugly, but I suspected both. Something--likely a weapon--bulged under his jacket near his waist.

"We're going to school, sir," I answered. "As you can see, we are wearing uniforms, not fishing gear." I joked, gesturing with my head towards the pier and holding his bloodshot gaze.

"I see you have a clever mouth," he said. "Try shutting up."

"Why would--," I began.

"Please, Patrick, stop!" Joyce tugged on my shirt.

"What can we do for you, sir?"

"Good girl," the man said. "I need to borrow your bicycle."

"No, sir," I replied, shaking my head. "I have a very important examination starting in an hour and my father would not want me to lend out his bike."

"Your father and I are friends," the man said in a friendly tone, spreading his massive arms innocently.

"I have never seen you," I said. "Say both his names."

"Stop wasting my time and hand over the bicycle!" The man's voice flipped into anger. His eyes widened, his nostrils flared, and he lunged towards us.

Fear froze my joints, but I clung tightly to the bicycle. The girls squealed and jumped to the ground. For a split second I wondered what was more dangerous: this man's wrath, or my father's if I lost his only bicycle.

Pulling at my shirt from where they hid behind me,

the girls whispered pleas for me to give up the bicycle. I shook my head and stood my ground.

In one motion, the man seized the bike's handlebars and flipped open his jacket to produce a pistol. Without flinching, he levied it at my head. "Let go, now!" he ordered.

The sharp screams of my sisters stabbed the air; I dropped the bike and raised my open palms. Dirty teeth bared, the man gave a final wave in the air with his gun. He leapt on the bike and began to pedal away, back towards my home. With barely a moment's hesitation, I took off after him. I knew that if he'd wanted to kill me, I'd already be dead.

This part of the road, awash with water and deep sand, was slow going on a bicycle. It didn't take a minute to catch up.

"At least allow me to come with you, so I can bring it back," I called, as I pulled alongside him.

"How stupid," he spat, hunched over the handlebars and pedaling furiously. Sand sprayed out behind the rear wheel as he hit a harder patch.

Taking his non-violent reaction as a go-ahead, I jumped onto the bike's rear carrier. I guarded my chin and head with my elbows like a boxer, anticipating retaliation. But nothing happened. He just moved his pistol into the front pocket of his jacket, out of my reach. The imminent fear of being killed diminished, and as I settled in for the ride I stole a glance behind me. Robinah was on her knees in the middle of the road, praying. Joyce simply stood there, arms hanging limp at her sides.

As we approached my home, I entertained a brief hope that my father or one of my uncles would see us and come to my rescue. Then I considered that the man was armed--and built like a bull. Perhaps it was better that they not see us. We passed two fishermen on bicycles and I considered calling out for help, but the same quandary stopped me--I didn't want to put unarmed citizens at risk.

I reluctantly narrowed my options down to one simple hope: that the man would have mercy and give the bicycle back. As my mind settled, I became very conscious of the nauseating odor of rotting vegetation and cigarette smoke radiating from his body. I squirmed to move as far away from his stinking, steaming form as possible.

"If you are planning anything back there, be warned," he hissed+. "I do not need to waste a bullet on you. I will twist your head off like a chicken, and throw it in the jungle for the foxes."

"I have no plans," I said. "I am only waiting for you to be finished borrowing my bicycle, so I may return it to my father for you."

He let out a hyena's laugh. "Don't joke with me."

A few kilometers further on, in the midst of the tangled jungle, the man pulled to a stop. I jumped off as he laid the bike down.

He walked a couple steps away and unzipped his pants to relieve his bladder, keeping heavy-browed eyes levied on me. I knew that this was my moment to escape.

"Your eyes tell me you are thinking about something," he said. "Don't do it!"

I waited until he was mid-stream. Then, with a pounce, I grabbed the bicycle and took off, pedaling with all my strength.

"Stupid boy!" he cursed, zipping up his pants. "You are going to make me shoot you!"

Taking his threat into consideration, I swerved off into the bush, hoping the thick vegetation would protect me from his bullets. The going was slow, and logs lay across my path. Suddenly, the bicycle was ripped out from under me. I pitched forward, landing hard on my side.

As I struggled to push myself up, a huge foot came crushing down on my abdomen.

"What a convenient place to kill you," he

threatened, brandishing his pistol. Little bits of spit flew from his rotted teeth as he sneered down at me. "I don't have to hide your body."

"Don't shoot, take the bicycle," I cried, raising the hand that wasn't pinned beneath me to shield my face.

He pressed his foot harder into my stomach as he waved the pistol. I felt my ribs against my lungs and struggled to suck in a breath as all his weight came crushing down on me. "If you mess with me again, I swear . . ."

With those words, he took the bicycle and left. The sound of the creaking gears fell quickly to the jungle. Soon, I could hear only the pounding of my heart and the wind wheezing as it passed through the towering trees. I lay for a minute, eyes closed, sucking in breath. The sun glinted through the leaves above, leaving a red image of my assailant painted across my eyelids.

Limping out of the jungle took all my energy. My

legs threatened to collapse. As soon as I reached the road I sank down against a rotting log. Tears of anger and frustration forced their way from my eyes. I couldn't return home without my father's bicycle--I couldn't give up yet.

Steeling myself against the pain that rocketed through my ribs with each breath, I pushed myself up and set off down the road. I followed the road to Kasokwe, the next trading center. He would not go unnoticed in our small community.

At the town, my suspicions were confirmed—every person I asked said they had seen a man fitting the thief's description heading toward a nearby fishing bay. I said he'd stolen my bike, and asked that they please report the incident to the military police should they see any. I cast my eyes up and down the dirt road, but its mirage and the tangled vegetation promised nothing. I could search for hours, and then what? My fists alone would do little against the burly thief.

With a reluctant sigh, I began the ten-kilometer trek back home.

Fifteen minutes down the road, a blue Toyota truck came speeding towards me. Vehicles were uncommon on these roads. Worried it might be another unfriendly stranger, I dashed into the forest.

The pick-up pulled to a stop. "Patrick!" a voice called. "Son! It is me!"

It was my father, surrounded by four military men. I recognized one of them as his good friend, Lieutenant Kisingiri. For a moment I hesitated, thinking about the punishment that awaited me for losing the bicycle. I knew that my sisters must have told him of the incident.

"Patrick, don't be scared!" My father called, as if reading my mind. "Please, come here. It's me!"

I walked out of the forest and approached the pick-up.

"Okay, Dada," I consented. "I'm sorry I lost your

bicycle."

"It's okay, son. Get in. We are going to find the man who stole it."

The men squeezed close together in the truck's small cab to make room for me. "You shouldn't have persisted in chasing that thief," Dada scolded, as we sped towards Kasokwe. "He is a dangerous man, on the run; he could have killed you! And for what, a mere bicycle?"

Afande Kisingiri nodded grimly and continued, "Even before your father reported Sergeant Ntege for stealing his bicycle, he was wanted for having deserted the army, reportedly to join a rival group. A heavy punishment awaits him."

"Ntege just added to his problems by stealing from your son. He could be charged for kidnapping him. Don't worry, we'll get him," Kisingiri added, rubbing the barrel of his gun.

With the soldier's accusation of Ntege, I decided it

was a kidnapping, and hoped he would get a severe punishment.

Because the suspected thief was trying to escape across Lake Kyoga, we searched the docks of a nearby village, then made our way down the shore, asking after him. At our fourth stop, a fisherman reported he had seen him just minutes ago at a dock up ahead.

We stopped along a bend in the road, out of sight of the bay. Kisingiri's men jogged silently away from the truck, surrounding the area.

"Stay in the truck," Kisingiri ordered me. "If there is any fighting, we don't want you around. From what your father told me, you attract trouble. John, stay behind me, you will be fine. Ntege is a coward."

Even though I was eager to help catch the criminal, I bit my lip to keep from reminding them of my military training and reluctantly followed the sergeant's instruction. After half an hour the men returned with Ntege, handcuffed and stripped of his shirt. Sweat shone over his bare torso, and his breath came in heavy rasps. He didn't make eye contact with me. One of the soldiers lifted him by his belt as they shoved him roughly into the back of the pick-up, forcing him down on his belly. The rest of the soldiers piled into the open bed, roughly propping their feet on him as if he were a footrest.

As my father and Kisingiri piled into the cab, they filled me in on the story. "My suspicions were right," Kisingiri said, pulling the truck into gear. "Ntege sold the bicycle and planned to use the money to negotiate transport across Lake Kyoga. Lucky for us, he stopped to flirt with a couple of prostitutes before securing his ride across. It was an easy catch, like a fish in shallow waters."

"The county chief found the money in his pocket and is going to use it to buy back our bicycle for us," Dada added.

News spread quickly through our small community.

When we arrived in Baale with the criminal, dozens of people were already gathered in the town square, including my mother, Baaba, and several of my uncles and aunties. They all cheered joyously as we pulled in, and the soldiers pulled Ntege up from where they had kept him prostrate beneath their feet.

"Let's lynch him!" someone shouted. People continued to pour into the square, and their yelling turned from joy into anger. Some began to demand that Ntege be handed over to them while others tried to poke at him with sticks, forcing the military officers to protect him.

Dada enjoyed the crowd, drinking beer and celebrating, I kept to the edges with my mother and grandmother. Mama wasn't her usual social self. Tears flowed occasionally from her eyes, and she stayed quiet, merely smiling at people in greeting. She followed me like a protective shadow, as if by letting me out of her sight, I would be taken away again.

After the celebration, father and I climbed back into the truck and drove with the soldiers and their prisoner down to the military police headquarters sixty kilometers away in Kayunga. At the station, Kisingiri handed the prisoner over to five guards. The young men fell upon him like dogs on a wounded antelope. As Kisingiri led us towards the station I stole a final glace behind me: Ntege curled into a ball, trying to protect his head and torso, while fists and feet flew at him from all sides.

We met the commander in a small, tidy office to fill out an incident report. "Sorry about your troubles today, Mr. Kalenzi," the commander said as we entered, shaking first my father's hand, then mine.

The officer's face looked strangely familiar.

"Sir, is your name Afande Kiwenda?" I asked, as he

took my hand in a firm military shake.

"Yes," he answered, looking at his chest, as if for a name tag. "How do you know me?"

"You registered me when I joined the NRA."

"Perhaps, I did," Kiwenda said, nodding thoughtfully and studying my face. "If your father is friends with Kisingiri, and is related to Gabo, then I'm sure it wasn't a coincidence that you ended up in the military with us. But what happened?" He raised his eyebrows and half smiled.

"You mean today or with the military?"

"We will talk about today in a moment," he said, waving dismissively. "I mean the military."

"I was injured."

"I am sorry to hear that." He gave me a look, then took a deep breath and shuffled some papers on the desk. "Well, why don't you tell me what happened today."

After the afande took down my story and assured us

that military law would take its course, he studied me again.

"I remember you now, Patrick Kalenzi. I heard of your unfortunate accident. From the fight you put up today, it is clear that you are well-healed. We could use a good soldier. When will you come back and join us?"

A surge of warmth filled my head. "Maybe I could--." I started, but Dada interrupted.

He smiled warmly at the officer and said, "We may get back to you, sir."

*   *   *

"Son, I had a drink down at the station today with Lieutenant Kisingiri," Father said at dinner later that week, spooning posho from a ceramic bowl. "He sends his greetings."

"That's nice of him, Dada," I replied. "It was very

kind of him to help us last week. He is a good soldier."

"Speaking of good soldiers..." Dada said, then paused, studying the maize on his plate very critically before clearing his throat and leveling his gaze at me. Mama had dropped her plate to her lap and sat frozen with her eyes pinned on him, but he pretended not to notice. "He believes you are capable of rejoining the military and getting a good rank because of your bravery and quick mind. He--."

"Stop right there, John."

Fury darkened my mother's face as she leaned towards him, her spine stiff, her strong, lanky arms braced upon her thighs. "You just can't help but to push this boy into further danger, can you?"

"The war is over, Florence. This is professional army recruitment and he would do well." He cleared his throat again and added, "They also provide young soldiers free education at the Kadogo Military schools."

Mama pushed her half-full plate aside, and wiped her hands shaking her head with disdain.

"Why can't you just admit that you don't want to pay for his school?" she spat.

"Florence, his education will only get more expensive from here on," Dada said. "And what about the other nine children?"

"Well, perhaps instead of wasting half our money drinking, you could save it for their schooling," she replied, gesturing at his half-full glass of gin with an angry hand. "That would be a good start."

"Wife . . . don't talk to me like that," Dada warned.

"I will talk to you anyway I choose when it concerns my children," she replied, spreading her arms like a bird protecting its fledglings.

Dada pushed his plate aside and stormed out of the house.

"Kids, finish your dinner and go to bed," Mama

commanded, her eyes fixed on the door. She took a deep breath, then pushed herself up and followed my father.

*   *   *

I was half finished milking the cows the next morning when my father came out, scratching his head and squinting in the weak morning light.

"I can finish the milking, Dada," I told him. I'd found myself doing all the morning chores lately, and had adjusted my schedule accordingly. This morning, I was also hoping that the gesture would soften him into telling me the outcome of his and mama's argument about my schooling.

"It's cold out here. Why aren't you wearing a sweater?" he asked.

"It is?" I said, glancing up at the clear sky and shrugging my shoulders.

"I don't mind if you want to do all the chores this

morning," he replied, changing the subject again. He stretched and leaned against the fence to watch me work. The milk steamed as it tinkled into the metal pail. "Soon, I'll be doing them all myself."

"Why?" I asked, dropping the cow's teats as a wave of something between panic and excitement hit me.

"You are going to move to the city for school. You'll live in Kampala with your half-brother, John Higiro."

"School in the city? I hear they are so much better than they are here! But half-brother?" I asked, confused. I didn't know I had a brother.

"John is the son your mother had before she married me. Didn't we tell you about him before?" Dada seemed to be asking himself more than me. "Anyway, come inside as soon as you're done. Once everyone is sitting down for breakfast, we will give you the details."

I finished milking as quickly as I could,

overflowing with excitement at the idea of going to a city school. My friend Ronald, who lived in the capital city of Kampala, had told me all about the big multi-level buildings, with their sprawling libraries and shining laboratories. The blessing of getting to live with this brother I'd never heard of only added to my happiness. I could barely keep from shaking as I raced in to take a seat across from my father on the cow-hide mats spread on the floor.

"Florence, why don't you start?" Dada suggested, sipping his cup of chai tea.

"We are going to send you to the city," Mama said with a warm smile. "Your father already told you, right?"

"Yes," I answered, beaming.

"Remember my sister Jona?" Mama asked.

I nodded.

"Last time I visited, I asked Auntie Jona if you could stay there," Mama said. "She said she was happy to house and feed you as long as we paid your school fees. My son John Higiro lives with her as well."

"I know John Higiro," Joyce piped in. "He came to visit once."

"Yes," Dada said. "But Patrick was quite young."

I was shaking so badly I spilled some of my chai.

"How old is John?" I asked.

"He is seventeen, three years older than you," Mama answered, "But you will have plenty of time to learn about him yourself when you meet him this weekend."

"This weekend? I'm moving to the city this weekend?" I asked, jumping off my seat and squealing like a pig. "What will I need?"

"You won't need much," Dada said, his lips retreating from a smile. "What I need is to find money to pay those school fees. Time to sell another cow." In the silence that followed, he pushed himself up and left the house.

Twelve

February, 1987 (Kampala, Uganda)

Umujyi *(the city)*

It took my father and me six hours and three mini-buses to reach Kampala. Though designed to hold just over a dozen passengers, many more crammed into the rickety old vehicles. The van's old shocks sagged and its engine roared angrily as it lurched along, people jumping in and out through the open door and balancing precariously along the glassless windows. The smell of sweat, jackfruit and the occasional whiff of livestock permeated the air. I stood spread-legged to keep my balance, with a firm grip on the small metal suitcase containing my meager belongings.

As we closed in on the capital, the world outside and inside the bus began to change. Dusty dirt roads withruts gave way to smooth pavement; the familiar-feeling clusters of old grass-roofed huts were replaced by strips of brick-walled shops, and then thick, towering multi-storied buildings. Even the passengers changed, from chicken-carrying farmers wearing simple, time-dulled cotton, to middle-class office workers dressed in clean, pressed slacks and elegant tops covered in rich designs.

Auntie Jona lived in Bwaise, a suburb about 5 kilometers north of Kampala city. Stepping off the commuter bus to walk the final hundred meters to her house, I was immediately overwhelmed by the sights and sounds of the unfamiliar urban bustle. Cars, a rare sight even in Baale, flew past in reckless droves, as frightening as a herd of stampeding cattle. Vendors filled the air with their shouts and smells. Some stood over trays of fried fish and chicken that they handed out in paper bags, others tended charcoal fires where they charred meat and then speared it on sticks. A few shouted over burlap sacks overflowing with dried beans, grains, salted fish, and spices in a vibrant rainbow of colors and textures. Beneath a hutch a little ways back from the road, an old woman hidden behind long veils and cloaks squatted beside a fire, stirring a cauldron of thick chai tea that she ladled into plastic cups. All I could see were her thin hands.

As we made our way through the crowd and up the hill to our destination, Dada prepped me with his limited bit of *Umujyi*, city savvy. "These drivers are scrambling for passengers; they don't pay much attention to pedestrians," he warned as a taxi flew perilously close to where we stood waiting to cross the street.

"Keep walking," Dada urged when a man descended upon us, grabbing our hands and battering us with pleas to inspect his wares. "Some of them are pickpockets pretending to be vendors."

The city's infrastructure mirrored its human chaos. Potholes and cracks miredthe tight roads. The sidewalk here was just a dirt path. Buildings of all shapes and colors sprang up without pattern or plan. On one side of the street, I saw a structure with a collapsed roof fallen; on the other rose a series of red brick houses with half-finished walls. Some shops seemed to lean over into the street, while others were pushed back off the path, fronted by pounded dirt and a few clumps of grass.

Occasionally, we passed sprawling mansions with manicured grounds kept behind towering sharp-toothed metal fences or concrete walls topped with rusting spools of barbed wire.

As we neared Auntie Jona's house, the carts of merchandise disappeared, and the spicy aromas of the street food gave way to the smell of sewage and exhaust, interrupted briefly by the sweet, toxic odor of a dog lying dead and bloated by the roadside. Just past the dog, we saw the problem: a broken pipe leaked a small, smoking stream of waste. Nostalgia for the fresh jungle scents of home came over me. Images of the blooming trees and flowers back in Baale, of Baaba, my sisters, and my dog lounging lazily beneath the mulberry tree flitted through my mind, but my intense urban reality drove them away. This would be my life for the next three months, possibly the next six years. I covered my nose and pushed on up the hill.

*   *   *

Auntie Jona lazed on a flimsy plastic chair outside her house, seeking shelter from the sun beneath an old Balboa tree. When she spotted us, she heaved herself up and sauntered over to wrap my father in a long hug. "Good to see you again, John," she said, pulling her shiny, red-painted lips into a smile.

"Good to see you too, Jona," Dada replied. "You haven't changed a bit; you look even better than the last time I saw you."

"Thank you," she said. "If your wife, who is six years younger than me, would have had fewer kids, she would look this good too!" she teased. They both laughed, Jona's bulging sides jiggling. The joke did not amuse me; this huge woman, with her overflowing hips and swaying rear looked nothing like my lanky, lithe mother. Softness defined Auntie Jona's features, and while she was not bad looking, there was nothing of my mother's clear, angular beauty.

Auntie Jona turned to me. "Look at how much you resemble my sister!" she exclaimed, cupping her large hands about my head before pulling me into a hug.

While utteringa muffled greeting, I went about trying to extract myself from the embrace without appearing impolite. The smell of her artificial flower perfume mixed with fresh liquor was oppressive up close.

"Oh, and he has our brother's ears!" Auntie Jona said as she pushed me away and gave one of my ears a squeeze. She went on exclaiming about my various physical attributes as she led us back to beneath the Balboa tree, gesturing towards a cluster mismatched chairs set around an old table. There were stools scattered about as well, and small tables here and there.

"A glass of juice for you, Patrick?" Jona asked.

"Yes, please," I answered.

She reached over from her chair to lift the top off a cooler filled with bottled drinks floating in water, and pulled out a half-full bottle of juice. Condensation beaded on the outside of the glass she filled with the thick orange liquid. I could feel my mouth begin to water: a cold drink was an unusual treat.

"Thank you, Auntie!" I said, carefully taking the glass from her stubby fingers. My mouth filled with the bright taste of mango and guava, and I closed my eyes to savor it.

When I opened them, I saw Auntie Jona smiling at me. "You just let me know if you would like some more," she said.

"And how about you, John? May I get you a cold beer?" she asked, turning towards my father.

"Of course!" My father replied. "Do you remember the good old times, when we had beer for breakfast and lunch?" he added, flashing a faint smile.

She opened a bottle with a refreshing *pop*. My father rubbed the sweating glass across his forehead, and they fell into conversation.

I learned how Auntie Jona made her living when a scrawny, pale man came by and asked to buy a glass of hard liquor. She sold beer, wine, and whisky from the little cart, mostly to local Rwandese. I would later learn that she also rented out rooms in her house and sold pancakes and various grocery items from a small room whose over-sized window opened up to the street. My future would hold many days behind that window, portioning off sugar, buns, soap, and other items from large sacks and trays for our small but loyal clientele.

The Rwandese customers fell into small talk with Auntie and Dada as they sipped their beverages. I found myself growing restless. As if reading my mind, Jona turned to me and said, "Go ahead and put your luggage inside. You'll be sharing the middle room with your brother—he should be home soon. In the meantime, make yourself comfortable." She pointed in through a cracked window at the main room.

The door hinge squealed when I opened it. Inside the plastering was unfinished, showing red bricks and mortar in broad swaths. Mismatched strips of linoleum covered parts of the cement floor, but were mostly jagged and cracked through. The front door opened straight into the multi-purpose room where I'd be living. Low twin beds with thin, lumpy mattress lay along two of the walls, and I had to walk around a large dining table to reach them. In one corner, a big cushioned chair with stuffing peeking out of one of its arms slumped next to a stained wooden side table topped by a kerosene lantern. I looked about for an electric light, but saw only slivers of sun coming through holes in the sheet metal roof.

I found a small closet half-filled with boys' clothing, and set about to unpack my few garments onto an empty shelf. When I opened my suitcase, the rangy, wild smell of sun-cooked ghee greeted me. Horrified, I pulled out my sandals, a toothbrush, a text book, and my two carefully folded outfits. All were covered in the stinking, clinging fat. I searched the case for its origin, and found a burst plastic bag still half-filled with melted butter. Mama or Dada had slipped it in without me noticing, no doubt as a thoughtful reminder of home. All I could think about was how unfortunate it was that cattle odors had followed me here, to my new life in the big city. Old memories of Muwonge's school yard teasing rose painfully into my consciousness.

"I can't be teased for smelling of cattle anymore!" I said out loud, wiping my hands disdainfully on a clean corner of one of my stained shirts. "I will wash these until my hands bleed!"

Dusk began to obscure the corners of the unlit room. I pushed my case under a bed and went out on the back veranda, perched over the hill. From the high outlook, I could see all the way to Kampala, where tall buildings glowed high into the sky. Sunlight was giving way to a full moon. A line of cars flashed red and white along the road to the capital. Hidden by darkness, the disrepair of Auntie Jona's neighborhood slowly gave way to scattered lights, sparkling a little like fireflies in the rolling savannah.

I must have stood for a long time, awed by the

sight. At some point, Auntie Jona appeared at my shoulder. "Are you looking for something?" she asked.

"No Auntie, I'm just watching the city, admiring it."

"Oh, I know why you're out here: it's so dark in the house. You're polite to say you are admiring the city."

"No, Auntie," I answered meekly. "It really looks like a million twinkling lights down there."

She gave me a smile and said, "Dinner will be ready soon, but would you like a snack before that?"

"No, thank you."

"Ha! A snack?" I heard Dada snort from inside. "This is new to his lifestyle. We sometimes have only one meal a day."

"Well then, I will put some meat on his skinny body," Auntie Jona said, and walked back into the house with another one of her belly-shaking laughs. I followed.

I heard the front door creak open.

"Oh good," Auntie Jona sighed. "Here comes soccer

boy."

My eyes adjusted to the yellow light of the kerosene lanterns, and I could make out a lean boy not much taller than I, dressed in black shorts and a bright red T-shirt. His ears stuck out just like mine. A woven plastic soccer ball spun in one of his hands, and he eyed auntie Jona cautiously, as if she might bite him.

"John, your brother has been here since three. Where in the world have you been?" she scolded, and I heard a new bite to her voice, as well as the slight slurring of liquor.

"With friends," John answered. "I'm sorry."

"Don't worry about it," she said, leaning on a chair with one hand while gesturing me forward with another. "Meet Patrick, who I told you was coming to live with us."

"Hello, Patrick."

"Hello, John."

We stood awkwardly staring at each other until

Auntie Jona said, "Is that all you have to say to each other, after all these years? Boys will always be boys . . . Anyway, John, make sure Patrick is settled in. I'll be back with food in a minute."

Auntie Jona banged out of the house, and I heard a peel of laughter echoing between her and Dada and the other customers who lounged outside on the plastic chairs. My brother dropped his ball and strolled over to perch on one of the beds.

"Sorry," he said. "She didn't tell me you were coming, or I would have been home earlier. Our team won a tough match today, and we hung out for a while after to celebrate. Do you play soccer?"

"Seldom, and I'm neither good at nor crazy about the sport," I admitted.

"Oh, just you wait, I will teach you tricks, and before you know, you will be hungry to show them off. It is a lot of fun!" he said, a smile lighting his face.

"So, is that your bed?" I asked.

"Yep. I imagine you'll sleep in that one," John instructed, pointing to the one I'd already placed my suitcase under. "It's usually a guest bed, but . . ." he ended with a shrug.

"Where does Auntie Jona sleep?" I asked.

"Hmm, that is if she sleeps," John joked. "After selling her alcohol and getting drunk with her customers, she goes to her bedroom, that one to the right," he indicated a closed door, then pointed to the one beside it "And that one she rents out," he explained.

John and I fell easily into conversation. I told him about my family, my brief stint with the military, and my recent kidnapping. He briefed me on soccer, city life, and the school we'd hopefully soon be attending. Too soon, Auntie Jona called us out for dinner, and our conversation paused as we turned to the steaming plates of *Matooke*, mashed banana, topped with peanut sauce. Long after John and I had cleared the dinner dishes and headed to bed, I could hear Dada and Auntie Jona out on the veranda, their voices and laughter growing louder as they emptied glass after glass of alcohol.

*   *   *

My father left for home early the following Monday morning. I had just gotten up and was getting dressed in my old school uniform of Khaki shorts and a white shirt when he came in the room to say goodbye.

"Don't you want to see where I will be going for school?" I asked.

"Son, I never went to school and don't know anything about it. Let your brother and auntie guide you. I must go take care of the family."

John and I walked Dada out to where the mini-bus had dropped us off only a few days earlier. The bus swerved to the corner and he hugged us tightly, then jumped aboard before it could leave without him. He hung out the door, waving a final goodbye and disappeared into traffic.

Back at the house, John and I shared a cup of tea and bread with butter before starting the five-kilometer walk to school. Before we left, John went into my aunt's room and got the envelope containing my school fees.

"Auntie wants me to take you to my school and see if they will admit you." he told me as we started down the hill towards Kampala. He waved the envelope and added, "We'll need this."

"Why doesn't Auntie Jona come with us?" I asked. "Dada said she would help."

"She is too sleepy and probably still drunk from last night," John said, wrinkling his nose. "To be honest, she wouldn't come even if she were sober. I don't think she values school at all. She's not educated herself!"

The walk to school passed quickly. As we passed through the slums, John explained what I'd encounter on my first day; the crowded classrooms, the long wait at the registrar's office, the guards at the gates. "One of them is an ex-soldier from Idi Amin's regime," he told me. "But he's illiterate, so Mr. Zubairi, the chemistry teacher, has to be there to read the pass slips and IDs. No one is allowed in without the right papers, unless they are on their way to get them."

"Why are they so strict about keeping people out of a school?" I asked.

John gestured at the dilapidated houses we were weaving between. Kids clad in clothes more threadbare than mine watched us with steady eyes.

"There are many kids in this city who would like to go to school but can't afford the fees," he said. "They will try to sneak in if they can. So we have fierce guards and a razor-wire fence to keep them out."

I had never seen so many kids in one place as at Kampala High. Khaki and white ruled the pavement as they filed in past the guards, IDs and passes waving. Ahead, the two-story brick building loomed broad and sturdy.

"My brother is here to apply for admission. May he go to the registrar's office?" John asked the skinny, shabbily dressed chemistry teacher as he presented his identification. The teacher checked the documents and waved us towards a long line of students.

The sheer mass of kids seeking admission was daunting. "Do you think they will accept me?" I asked John.

"Why wouldn't they?" he replied. "Look at all those students. You think they all have better grades?"

"You know . . . I'm coming from a village school and all . . ."

"This school will take a mentally disabled person if they pay fees," John assured me.

"Of course, as a result, the classes are all full past capacity," he continued. "Kampala High has so many students; they split the school into morning and afternoon sessions."

A short man, with stunted limbs and an oversized head approached us with his hand extended.

"Previous school report, please," he said.

He took the slip of paper in his stubby hand and squinted briefly down at the small print. "Very good. Did you bring your fees?"

"Yes, sir, my brother has them," I said.

"Fill out this form and bring it back. You'll be given a deposit slip. Bring it to the bank with your fees."

"Does this mean I am accepted?" I asked. A moment that had seemed so profoundly important and intimidating had just slipped by.

"Yes, of course," the man said, and he moved down the line to the next boy, arm still extended.

* * *

My first semester at Kampala High breezed by. Despite the substandard level of education I'd received at the village school, I adjusted quickly. Though the expected level of performancewas higher than in Baale, the quality of schooling seemed dismal. The classrooms overflowed with kids squeezed into any space they could find. They perched on desks and sills, and even stood outside and leaned in through the open windows when the room was too far past capacity. Some of the children, like me, were straining their family's budget to be there, and we paid as rapt and close attention to the lessons as we could. Unfortunately, too many of the students were totally uninterested, treating the classroom like a playground. The teachers themselves, overworked, underpaid, and with class sizes too large to manage, approached their work with bitterness. They taught without enthusiasm, and often showed up late or even not at all, leaving us to sit waiting until the class period ended.

Even though my reputation as a soldier didn't protect me as it had in Baale Primary, John made sure that no bullies targeted me, and the two of us became fast friends. He served as my personal tour guide to the city, taking me to visit museums, to peer through the windows of the fancy downtown shops, and to see my first movie in a theater. As promised, I soon developed a taste for soccer, and we spent many hours dribbling the ball and practicing tricks in the alleyways we walked through on our way to and from school.

Life with Auntie Jona was pleasant enough at first—she smothered me in motherly attention for my first several weeks, and insisted on feeding me heaps of food. Though her cooking wasn't as good as my mother's, it was nice to always have a cold cup of juice or plate of hot posho nearby. However, with time, and because she wasn't getting enough money from my parents to house and feed me, her attitude towards mechilled. John and I spent as much time as we could away from the house and the shady clientele always moving in and around it.

What began as normal chastising, Auntie Jona's barrage of insults, complaints and grumbles continued throughout the semester. If it wasn't for school, and my brother's good character and friendship, I would have given up and returned home. When the term came to an end, I was happy to return home. I hoped that my parents would have a better plan.

Thirteen

1988 (Kampala, Uganda)

Imicomyiza (good manners)

From the moment I stepped off the mini-bus into a different suburb called Najjanankumbi, I knew I'd be better off there than in Bwaise. Though father and I were bombarded by the regular city rush of street vendors hawking their commodities and beggars pulling at our sleeves, the air didn't smell of sewage. I noticed immediately that there was less garbage piling up along the street gutters. While in Auntie Jona's neighborhood, men lounged along the street corners in drunken disarray at all hours, the people here were dressed professionally and appeared to be going about important matters of business.

I followed Dada up a path, weaving away from the vendors and into a more residential area. As we walked, Dada gave me a brief history of his cousin. Baaba's sister— my uncle Yosia's mother—died right after the family fled Rwanda during the 1959 Tutsi expulsion. During the turmoil of the exodus and subsequent resettling in Uganda, my grandfather played a vital role in providing shelter, food, and protection to Yosia and his family. After that, Yosia always regarded Baaba as a father.

"His current work has something to do with the schools, so perhaps—" Dad's thought trailed off as an elfin middle-aged woman with mushrooming afro hair stepped out from behind a grocery kiosk and came towards us.

"You must be going to Yosia's house," she said, extending a hand towards my father. "Are you related?"

"Yes, he is my cousin," Dada replied, tentatively

accepting her handshake. "How did you know we were going to see him?"

"It is obvious you are Rwandese," she said, and flashed a grin. "Being Rwandese as well, I can tell. In this area, almost all Rwandese who come through are here to visit Yosia. He is well known here for his *imicomyiza*."

"Miss, can I buy some bananas?" a young boy dribbling a soccer ball interrupted.

"Yes, yes," she answered. "But first let me help these men." She turned back to us. "You need to go back and take the other path," she said pointing south. "It will take you straight to Yosia's home."

"What happened to this one?" Dada inquired, pointing west, the way we were walking.

"Ha! A rich man built his mansion across it— illegally, of course. And no matter how much we complained, the town council allowed it. You know what money can do in our country."

"Oh I do," Dada commiserated, rolling his eyes.

We bade the kind little woman farewell and headed back towards a narrow road that wove between pine trees and a tall brick wall. After fifty meters or so, the wall made a right angle, and we emerged onto another street. Other than their well-kept grounds and general neatness, there seemed to be little cohesion in the houses around us—they varied drastically in shape, size, and value.

Dada led us up the front path of a modest brick home, literally overshadowed by big newer houses on either side. A charcoal cooking stove smoked in the small, well-kept yard. Neighbors watched us idly from their shaded verandas.

Dada raised his hand to knock at a door frame hung with a faded green curtain, but before he knocked, a light-skinned woman slid the fabric aside.

"John, what a surprise!" The woman stepped over the door sill. "Good to see you both!"

After hugging my father, she wrapped her arm around my shoulder and introduced herself as my aunt Edith.

"Is Baba getting too old?" Edith inquired, serving us cool water from a pitcher and inviting us to sit on the *mukeka*, a traditional multi-colored hand-woven mat, laid out in the shade of a tree.

"His mind is as sharp as ever," Dada replied, "but he's finally succumbing to old age. He can't see or hear very well, and his body is no longer strong these days." A hint of sadness creased my father's face.

Darkness fell as we sat outside, chatting with Edith and her children as they trickled in from the streets. Uncle Yosia's house had no electricity, but a neighbor's security light flicked on, illuminating the yard. Uncle Yosia was the last to arrive, breaking into the halo of light with a smile already on his face. He was dressed professionally, and his bellybulged in a friendly and well-fed manner. He greeted

Dada and me with genuine warmth.

Edith ushered us into the house for a dinner of fried beans and sweet potatoes. I sat on a mat along the wall with the other seven children, while the adults sat around a small table. As Edith was coming around to clear our plates, Dada broached the subject of our visit.

"Patrick's auntie in Bwaise is not fit to house or feed him anymore, and I can't afford boarding schools. As you know, there are no facilities for higher education near our home." Silence fell over the room, and my father looked down at his hands. "I apologize for coming here with such a burden without prior warning, but you know we don't have a phone and I don't know how to write."

Uncle Yosia took a deep breath. "Hmm, John, this is quite a predicament," he said, clasping his chin in thought. "Baaba tells me Patrick is very bright; it would be a shame for him to drop out of school. But—" he gestured at the children filling the small house. My heart sank. But

357

Yosia caught his tongue and took a deep breath. "Kids, you should go outside for a while."

The next couple of hours passed with excruciating slowness. Yosia's eldest son took me out to a favorite overlook. The lights of the city twinkled below like gems just out of reach, and huge planes buzzed low overhead as they came and went from the nearby Entebbe airport.

"If you lived here, we could go down to the airport to watch the famous people board the planes," he said, then added proudly, "I've seen the Pope, Muammar Gaddafi of Libya, and many other dignitaries."

I smiled, but stifled any hopes that rose. Uncle Yosia seemed such a kind man, but their means were obviously meager, and their house already full. If supporting me had been too much for Jona, how could they possibly manage?

*   *   *

The other teenaged kids and I had fallen into low gossip over the flickering charcoal stove when Yosia finally called out that we could return to the house. A cloud of doubt hung over my head as I ducked into the dimly lit living room. Then, I made out the smile on my uncle's broad face, his kind eyes sparkling. He placed a hand on my shoulder, "Patrick, we would be pleased to receive you as one of our own. You can stay with us."

Relief filled me, but on its trail came a wash of fear—would this situation be any different from the last? Would I forever be a burden, pushed from one relative to another, dependent on fleeting generosity? I looked around the room, at the beaming faces of my cousins, the kindness and warmth of my aunt and uncle. As if reading my worries, Yosia added, "Your father only has to pay your school fees and I will take care of everything else, without demands or making you feel guilty. Ask me anything. Ask my wife for anything. Make this your home. You are part of our family now. "

I embraced my father and relatives in thanks. As Edith and John fell into discussion, and the children fell into celebrating having a new playmate, Uncle Yosia took me aside. "Your Baaba tells me of your dreams to someday attend Makerere University. These dreams may be lofty, but they are not impossible. However, the odds are stacked against you. Kampala High has a bad reputation, and not just for its academics. I wish we could help you attend a better school, but—" He shrugged with genuine regret, then continued, "If you work very hard for the next three semesters, and make use of the library and other facilities, you may be able to transfer to a better school for the last two years of upper secondary. But be aware—Kampala High is a school where it is easy to fall in with a bad crowd. And if you do so, your dreams will turn to dust."

Amahoro *(peace)*

My next two semesters at Kampala High flew by. Life with Yosia and his family was undemanding and a*mahoro,* peaceful. My uncle's words of warning faded as I continued to excel in all my classes. I began the last semester of my lower-secondary education at the top of my class, and took for granted that I'd earn high enough grades on my exit exams to secure a position at a more reputable school for upper-secondary—the critical two years that would determine whether I could earn admittance, and a much-needed scholarship to a university. Perhaps it was the ease with which I exceeded Kampala's unchallenging standards, or perhaps it was just the fact that I was a teenager, but something changed that third semester. First, I joined the boxing team. Then, I found my first girlfriend.

Shakira, with her graceful way of moving across a

361

room and her cobra-quick wit, was the belle of Kampala High. She was skinny as an alley cat, with dark skin and bright white eyes, and she commanded attention and obedience from the students that flocked around her like bees to a blossoming poppy. And like a poppy, with its intoxicating fragrance, her charms could have a dangerous effect.

"Can I share a table with you?" Those were the first words I ever spoke to her. After being back at Kampala High for two semesters, I'd settled in comfortably, and the cool February day had made me feeling confident. It was a Friday, and for some reason, Shakira sat eating lunch alone. She turned to me with a smile, then eyed the free tables around her. Embarrassed, I began a quiet retreat.

"Hey, you, stop." Shakira followed her words with a soft laugh. "It's okay, come and sit."

I turned around and walked back to her table. I was

half-smiling and half-gritting my teeth.

"You didn't have to ask me;" she said slyly, looking out from behind her long, dark lashes, "This table belongs to the canteen."

She put a bite of food in her mouth and chewed it slowly.

"Perhaps it was an excuse to talk to you," I replied boldly, fixing my gaze on her while I toyed with my plate of rice and stew.

"Stop staring at me, your meal is going to get cold," she ordered, narrowing her eyelids and stifling another giggle.

"As you say, your royal highness," I chided with a respectful sweep of my hand.

Our flirtatious banter continued as the lunch period wore on. Ten minutes before the bell for class rang, she excused herself from the table, leaving me to pretend to peruse her copy of Ebony magazine while I watched her saunter off, silken dark hair blooming on her head, short dress clinging to her body. She returned with two cold Fantas, sat down with a wiggle of her hips, and slid one across the table.

"For me?" I asked, truly surprised. Soft drinks were quite a luxury, and I hadn't had many.

"Sure," she said with a casual shrug.

As we sipped our sodas, she told me about her family with their sprawling estate overlooking the city, and spoke of foreign lands I'd only dreamed of—places like Bangkok, Rome, and the USA; she talked of them as if they were second homes. I kept her going as much as I could, and gave occasional half-truths about my history, not wanting to turn her off with my poor background.

The bell rang. She glanced up briefly but didn't make any move to get up. Following her cue, I pretended not to notice and took a sip of my soda. When the second bell rang signaling the beginning of class, I stood up, stretched, and gathered our plates.

"Thank you for letting me share a table with you," I said.

"Thank you for not being so annoying like most guys that talk to me," she replied, pushing herself up from the table to stand beside me.

"Does that qualify me to talk to you again?"

Shakira nodded and left me with a perfumed smile. I took a deep breath, then bussed our plates in a daze. I was one of the last students to make it to class, and had to sit on a back window, where I could barely hear the lecture over the chatting of those in front of me. A brief pang of guilt interrupted my swoon, but I justified my tardiness with the fact that it was a one-time glitch in my otherwise perfect track record. There was a cool breeze coming in the window, birds twittering musically outside, and the memory of Shakira's hand touching mine as she handed me that sweating Fanta . . . Soon all anxiety and attempts to make out the teacher's voice faded as my mind wandered off to a blissful place.

*   *   *

Shakira came from a rich family, and she shared her money generously. The luxuries it afforded us proved an irresistible distraction. As the months wore on and our relationship became more serious, I spent increasing amounts of time going out to watch movies at the theater and dance to live music, or skipping classes to take long lunches at restaurants downtown. Rather than taking walks through Makerere University to study and daydream on the green grass of its well-manicured quad, I found myself heading over to Shakira's shiny new bungalow to watch shows on her color television. When I wasn't hanging out with my new girlfriend, I was training with the school's boxing team, the sport I'd taken up shortly before meeting her and which I now threw myself into with vigor.

Between the two extracurricular activities, my

reputation and stature at Kampala High grew. Rigorous physical training made my body strong, Shakira's trickle-down wealth swelled my self-importance, and my place amongst the school's untouchable athletic elite laid to rest an anxiety about being bullied that had pursued me since Muwonge beat me up on my first day at Mr. Reuben's Village School. That some of my new friends were also the school's more notorious trouble-makers did not faze me. I was seventeen, and I felt invincible and perfectly in control. It would take two explosions to knock me back into reality.

The first came from a gun.

*　　*　　*

It was a sunny afternoon, but not too hot or heavy, the air was gentle and clear, and everyone was happy and hopping about, full of energy. After school, I stood chatting with some other students near the vendor kiosks, munching on a decadent lunch of *chapati*,a deep-fried dough pocket filled with cinnamon-spiced beef and peas. A woman's scream

367

ripped through the air.

"Help, help!" she cried. "Thieves! They are beating me and stealing my pancakes, Help!"

Without hesitation, I took off towards the commotion. As the scene of the ruckus came into view, my pace slowed and my mind struggled to find an appropriate response to the unfortunate scenario. The woman, still screaming that she was being beaten, held onto the shirt of Otto, one of my fellow boxers. Another female vendor had him by the belt, while a third struggled to keep the boxer's hand in her grip. Otto struggled to pull away, but the women held fast and continued to scream. There were no pancakes in sight, and by all appearances, Otto was the only person being assaulted.

"Let me go before I hurt you!" he finally yelled.

"Not until you pay. You will give me money, or you will go to jail!" threatened the woman.

Otto gave a heavy twist, freeing his left hand. He

swung his right under the chin of the woman who had been holding him, hitting her so hard she went sprawling backwards. Thus freed, he was able to swing both his elbows back; dealing sharp blows to the two women still clutching him from behind. They released him simultaneously, staggering, and he spat coolly into the dusty earth.

"Hey, man, what's going on?" I asked, clenching my fists nervously as I surveyed the stunned women. One clutched a bloodied nose; another was bent over trying to recover her breath. All sobbed in pained anger, though their words had disintegrated with the shock of Otto's blows.

Otto, glazed with adrenaline and sweat, ignored my inquiries and began to walk back towards the school grounds. Just past me, he spun on his heel to yell, "I pay you, but you accuse me of stealing? Ha! Who are you trying to fool?"

Students began gathering around, staring gape-mouthed at the swaggering boxer. Several of our teammates let out cheers of support. Just before Otto reached the school compound, two policemen, one a husband of one of the women, broke through the crowd in a full-out run, batons in hand. Otto spun to avoid being trapped in the schoolyard and took off at a full sprint.

Even though the pursuing officers had a start on him, he accelerated fast and began to pull away. The other boxers and I cheered wildly. Just when it looked like he'd escape into the winding labyrinth of the surrounding slums, a policeman jumped out at him from behind a wall and tackled him to the ground. I caught a glint of light reflecting off the pistol strapped to his side. The other officers closed in and soon all three were upon him like rabid dogs, fists, feet, and batons flying.

My moral hesitations fell away in a rush of adrenaline-spiked defensiveness at the sight of my fallen friend. With the rest of the boxers, I took off towards the fray.

The policemen were so caught up in their rage they didn't even hear us approach. The surprise of our descent stunned them briefly. They turned from the prone and bloodied Otto to vent their rage on us. Then, a shot rang out through the air.

The gravity of the situation ricocheted through my head with the dying echo of the gun. How had I ended up here? Time slowed as I backed away, realization spreading from the top of my head and down through my body like a haunting ghost. Senior four class finals were in one week, and I was in a gun-fight with the police—over pancakes. I hadn't even cracked my books to study.

I watched as the boxing team captain leapt from behind the armed officer, grabbing hold of the barrel of his gun. The weapon flashed wildly between them. The rest of the fighters raged on as if energized by the shot's vibrations. One of our teachers, an ex-military man, slammed his way towards the team captain and the cop todisengage the gun's magazine. Before the two could register that they were struggling for control of an empty weapon, the teacher had extricated himself and took off sprinting as though chased by demons. He made it to the nearby police station, turned over the bullets, and alerted them to the escalating situation. By the time a dozen more police arrived on the scene, their fellow officers were receiving a severe beating. The boxers, satisfied, took off running with shouts of victory, leaving behind three crumpled and moaning bodies. No one was arrested.

I stood for a long time at the edge of the school grounds, staring off in the direction the boxers had run, too wrapped in thought to move. That night, fueled by shame and the realization that I was woefully unprepared to take the most important tests to date of my scholastic career, I stayed up until midnight, studying by the flickering light of an oil lamp.

Fourteen

November, 1989 (Baale, Kampala & Kamwenge, Uganda)

Ishuri*(school)*

After finals, I returned home to Baale for Christmas vacation. The bus dropped me at Kiyange, a trading center near my house. My father was there, sitting on the porch of a bar, a tall glass of waragi in his hand. He was as surprised to see me as I was to see him. As I strolled across the patio, he squinted in my direction through alcohol-dulled eyes.

"*Nibite*, Dada," I called in greeting, waving.

"*Nibyiza. Nibitebyawe, Sha.*" He shifted as if to rise to greet me, but instead just looked me up and down, a slight smile lifting his puffy cheeks. "Look at you; you are almost as tall as I am! How is *ishuri* going?"

"School is okay," I lied. I couldn't help but stare back. His body, once lean and strong, was now gaunt and floppy beneath stained, awkwardly fitting clothes. A year ago, his collars were always starched and his pants, though worn, were scrubbed mercilessly and neatly pressed. Now, he looked little better than the bums who begged half-servings of Auntie Jona's most crude waragi.

Our exchange of pleasantries and news drifted into silence, as Dada's heavy eyes faded in and out from my face to somewhere far over my shoulder or deep in his glass. I invited him to walk home with me, but he declined.

Mama was taking an afternoon nap, but the noise my nine siblings made welcoming me home woke her up. She rushed into the yard to greet me. It had been a year since I had seen her, and she pulled me into an embrace so tight it was as though we'd been tied together by the vines of a fig tree.

Finally, she pushed me back and with shining eyes declared, "Girls, don't you think that Patrick has gained weight?"

"Who would've imagined a skinny boy like him would look normal!" Joyce answered with a big smile.

"Your uncle and Edith must be feeding you well," Mama said.

My littlest siblings clung to my legs, and the older ones fluttered around us like birds at a feeder as we walked to the shaded side of the house. Spread out before me were the pasture-fronted edges of the creeping jungle, the kicked-up paddock, the old mulberry tree dropping its staining fruit. Chickens chatted to each other in low clucks, a goat perched casually in a crooked old tree. The sun shone as ever through the tight ceiling of blue sky above, and the air carried that familiar rich scent of livestock, decay, and blooming things.

After being caught up on the family happenings, I excused myself and hurried towards Baaba's old grass-thatched house.

Inside, the old man reclined on his bed, the sinking afternoon light deepening the wrinkles on his leathery face. "Rwabagabo?" he ventured in a shaky voice, drawing open his mosquito net to peer at me through eyes that had seen enough for their lifetime and begun to cloud over.

I sat down on the bed to hug grandpa, after which he pushed himself up and insisted that we walk outside. I helped him to his feet and we made our way to the veranda, Baaba leaning on his thick old *inkoni* as if it were another leg. I recalled the day not long ago when he'd taught me to use that stick for protection against an attacker and to separate fighting bulls.

At dusk, Robinah's voice came echoing across the compound, calling us for dinner. Father was an uncomfortable absence at dinner, but we talked and carried on with a veil of normalcy until ten o'clock, when mama finally cleared her throat and asked with a faint smile if I remembered how to milk.

"C'mon Mama! I could sooner forget to eat," I replied.

Baaba laughed and slapped his hand weakly on his leg. "He's talking like a man now!" Our laughter trickled off.

"Is this . . . normal?" I asked my mother about dad.

She shrugged. "He often does not come home until after midnight. Sometimes the cows get milked, sometimes . . ."

Baaba interjected, "Something in your father has changed. He is overcome by alcohol."

I excused myself and went out to the paddock. To my surprise, only four cows stood there, sleepily chewing at their cud. When I returned, I asked my mother if all had been brought in from pasture today, and she nodded sadly.

"That's all we have left, Patrick. Your father's been selling them off one by one and exaggerating how expensive your school fees are. I'm not sure if he's trying to fool me or himself."

The three of us stayed up chatting until past midnight. When we finally finished our last cup of tea and I walked Baaba back to his house, my father had still not come home from the tavern.

*   *   *

The next day, I rose early to do the morning chores. My father wandered out of the house with a vague excuse for his absence and a half-hearted and bleary-eyed thanks. I stood for a while with the shrunken herd, wondering how much longer they could sustain my family—and my school fees. I wasn't the only one considering such things.

Later, after Mama and Baaba joined us, and as we all lounged under the old mulberry tree, the subject turned towards my education.

"Rwabagabo," Grandpa asked. "What is your plan?"

"You mean for school?" I replied.

"Is it true that you have finished secondary level?"

"Yes," I fudged, deciding not to mention the possibility that I had failed my exit exams and might need to repeat a semester. I knew that failing would almost certainly mean the end of their paying my school fees and perhaps the end of my education. It wasn't a possibility I was ready to think about yet. "I still have high school, which takes two years, and I intend to go to the university after that."

"My Rwabagabo!" Baaba exclaimed, slapping a gnarly hand to his old thigh. "You are the first one in our family to have such academic aspirations."

"Patrick," Dada interjected, "High school is not for

you; we definitely can't afford it."

"Why not?" I asked, the warmth of my grandfather's response replaced by cold fear.

"Our family has come this far without education. Your place is with the cattle. You have received enough of an education. What you need to do now is come home and help me take care of our family's herd." He spat into the dusty earth. "You are a Tutsi, a Rwandese refugee. This higher level education is not for us."

Shocked silence fell over the group. Grandpa shifted uncomfortably in his chair and opened his mouth, but my mother beat him to it.

"Don't you dare stifle his dreams by calling him a refugee. He is a citizen of this country by all definitions," she scolded. I waited for her to say something about the school fees. She didn't.

I took a deep breath. My eyes moved from my mother to Baaba, then came to rest on Dada.

"Dada, are you saying that you will no longer pay for my schooling," I said, choking on the words.

Baaba shifted his watery gaze towards his old hands. My mother's eyes bored into my father. He avoided eye contact with me and nodded stiffly.

I excused myself and walked away.

Simba, my devoted canine, old and grey now, with a split ear from some old fight and a limp, followed at my heels as I walked out to the cow paddock. I sank down into the fresh hay bedding of the calf pen, surrounded by the familiar smells. The old dog sat quietly at my side, and together we stared out at the place we'd always called home.

Nostalgia filled me, along with a sense of frozen time and stagnation. Life went on here, unchanging and predictable, yet subject always to the whims of others—a government that could kill us for being born of Rwandan blood, landlords that could take away the land we'd tended for a generation without warning or reason. If I succeeded in my studies, I could earn a living that could buy land for my family; I could move us out of the reach of the bloody hands of a racist government should their threats return. But if I failed… this was the future that lay before me. I could see it in my father's vacant gaze.

Umurimo *(job)*

The next morning I caught the first bus back to Kampala city. Uncle Yosia was polishing his shoes in the yard when I arrived. He put down a brown-stained rag and studied me kindly as I put down my small suitcase and sank into the old plastic chair beneath a shade tree.

"I don't mean to pry," he said, after we'd exchanged greetings, and I lingered in the yard, "but why are you back so early? It's not even Christmas yet."

"My family and I had a disagreement," I explained. "They will not pay for any more of my schooling."

"I am sorry to hear that," Yosia replied sadly. "I wish I could help, but as you know . . . I barely make enough to support my own kids."

"The mere fact that you allow me to live with your family is a huge sacrifice and has allowed me to attend school in the first place; I am forever grateful for that and would not ask for more."

We stood for a moment in the yard, discussing ways I might find *umurimo*, employment over the two-month break between school terms. The one hundred dollars I would need to cover my fees next semester seemed an impossible amount to earn in such a short time, but I pushed that thought out of my mind. If it took not sleeping for the next two months, working day and night until my fingers bled, I would find a way to fund my upper-secondary education.

*　　*　　*

I spent the next three weeks running errands for a growing

number of friends and neighbors of Yosia's. I didn't tell

Shakira or any of my boxing friends that I'd returned early

from Baale. All of my time went into working or looking

for more work; I fetched people's groceries, carried their

water from the city wells, picked up their prescriptions

from the pharmacies; I did whatever was needed. As time

wore thin until I needed to have my school fees earned, the

stack of bills I kept in my backpack barely seemed to grow.

As I picked up more jobs and ranged farther out into the

city, I spent increasing amounts of money on transportation

fees, and my profits barely seemed to increase with relation

to my workload. There was no way I'd be able to earn

enough money like this. I had to find a better way.

One day, while shuttling heavy loads of water from

the community pump to my neighbor's house, I mentally

reviewed the work habits of my peers. I cringed to think of what my friends from the boxing team did to earn money, and pushed that thought out of my mind. My brother John still received support from his father, and Shakira never had, and probably never would, work a day in her life. I was just beginning to despair of this exercise bearing any fruit when I recalled a story my old friend Ronald related a year or so ago while we were watching movies at his uncle's house. I'd asked him where he'd found the money to buy the flashy new pair of Nike's on his feet, and he'd told me about taking a train to Western Uganda to buy potatoes, then bringing them to Kampala to sell on the streets for a profit. Perhaps I could try something similar. It seemed a long shot, but my time was running short, and my ideas were running dry.

As soon as I finished my day's work, I headed over to Nsambya, the suburb where Ronald lived with his uncle. We chatted for a while about soccer and school. I told him that my parents couldn't pay for my A-level education and that I was working as many odd jobs as I could get to try to afford it myself.

"That's not going to work," Ronald said bluntly, shaking his head.

"I know. That's why I have come to you."

"You are remembering my potato trafficking scheme," he said with a sly smile.

I nodded, trying not to look too eager. The fact that he'd suggested a business idea immediately filled me with hope.

"Well, if we went in on it together, you could earn yourself enough money to make a year of school fees in four or five trips. Which you could certainly get in before the semester begins. But there are two problems: my uncle doesn't work for the train any longer, so I can't get free tickets like I used to, and you need start-up capital to buy crops."

At the mention of money, I slumped in my chair. "How much will I need?"

"Depending on what crops you buy, it varies... but you could get off the ground with twenty US dollars. You'll want to invest more on subsequent trips, to increase your profit."

"Twenty U.S. dollars?" I exclaimed, nearly dropping my glass of chai tea. "How can I get that?" I found myself thinking forlornly of the twenty-five dollars hidden under my bed.

Ronald shrugged. "I already have my half. We can start as soon as you get yours together. Is there anyone you can borrow from?"

Once again, my thoughts flitted briefly to Shakira and to the boxers with their underhanded ways. I'd promised myself that those days were over; that I would no longer put my future at risk for temporary thrills and dead-end pastimes, that I'd follow the rules and keep out of trouble and away from the law. I didn't want to risk falling back into those habits—not when my education was already teetering in such a perilous way.

Sighing, I shook my head. "I'll find a way."

Then something occurred to me.

"Wait a second, what about train tickets? Do I have to save up to buy those, too?" I couldn't even afford to take a train home for break—this idea was beginning to strike me as hopeless.

Ronald smiled and a wicked gleam came to his eyes. "Oh, we'd never make a profit if we paid to ride the train," he said.

I was confused.

"So, how do we ride the train without paying?"

Ronald replied with a wink. "That's the fun part."

*   *   *

A few days later, I went to the local market to mail a Christmas card to my family. Guilt for having left so quickly on the heels of our unpleasant exchange clung to me. When I should have expressed gratitude for the years they had paid for my schooling, I'd thought only to berate them for leaving me to my own devices at a time when they were obviously struggling. I handed the letter to the postman with a heavy heart.

"Kalenzi?" he asked, reading my name from the envelope. "You have a letter."

I took the envelope, opening it as I walked out into the searing city heat. I expected chastisement for my hasty departure, but found something very different instead, scrawled in the rough script of my sister Robinah.

Dear Brother,

It is your sister, Robinah, once again doing secretarial work for Mama and Dada.

Before I tell you what they want me to write, I want you to know that your humble dog Simba died. I'm sorry. I'm also a bit worried about you. You left without pocket money or school fees.

Anyway, Dada wants to tell you that he holds no grudge; it is just that he can't afford your school fees any longer. That's really all he told me to write before he left for the bar. He drinks heavy these days.

Mama has been worried sick. She says she sold her mother's cow to help you with school, so you wouldn't do something drastic or stupid. Most important, she wants to make sure that you are neither going to be a street kid nor join the military again. She sent the money to your uncle Yosia.

Baaba seems to miss your company.

Make sure to write back soon, okay?

Your sister,

RobinahMirembe

Excitement battled sadness in my brain. I'd witnessed my father's deteriorating condition when I was home, but to see it on paper, in my sister's slow careful script, only increased its gravity. I felt a moment of hopelessness, a moment of regret for taking away from thedwindling herd, for not being home to care for my mother and my sisters and my aging grandfather. But what good would I really do them? It was like when I was a child, during the war. I could have stood beside my father as we hid in the jungle, ready to strike out with my little fists at the heavily-armed government militia that kept raiding us. Instead, I left my family to join the rebel forces; I put my strength in a place where I could make a difference, fighting for the army that could overthrow the tyrannical government and win freedom for my family and my people. The quick fix answer was seldom the best one. The best means I had to help my family was to get an education, so I could someday help buy them out of poverty. It first meant finding the funds to finish high school.

A cow would bring in close to a hundred dollars—not enough to pay a semester's school fees, but just what I needed to kick-start my potato trading business. There was still more than a month before the semester began; if

Ronald's estimations were accurate, that was time enough to earn a year's worth of school fees. If we could squeeze in an extra trip, I could save that money and use it to earn my fees again next year. My family would no longer need to worry about supporting me.

I rushed to alert Ronald that I'd found funding, then home to gather the money from my uncle. That night I barely slept, tossing between sweat-damp sheets as the risks and rewards of the next day's mission flitted through my head. If anything went wrong, my mother would have sold one of the family's most valuable assets for nothing. But if things went well, I'd be holding in my hands more money than I'd ever had and the ticket to my education.

*   *   *

By three the next afternoon, Ronald and I stood at a railroad crossing just past the station. On my back were four burlap sacks for carrying home my merchandise, rolled up tight so as not to draw attention. I felt nervous and itchy. The money burned hot in my pocket, and sweat dampened my hands. "So, tell me one more time how this works?"

Ronald rolled his eyes and let out an exaggerated sigh. "The train stops at the station where it loads its more traditional passengers—"

"You mean people with tickets," I cut in.

"Right—" Ronald waved off my comment. "It won't pick up speed until after it's gone through the crossing. Wait until the third to last car passes before you start running. Then, it's just a matter of grabbing a hold of the last car and jumping in. When you hit the floor of the car, roll to the corner. I'd go first, except the train will only pick up speed so—better if you do." He smiled and added, "Just you wait, it's a rush! Soon you'll be trafficking potatoes for the fun of it."

As if on cue, the train whistle cut through the air.

"Here we go!" Ronald whispered excitedly as a chugging sound rumbled through our chests and the massive machine drew closer, looming impossibly large. As the engine car roared past, I felt the breeze stir, and adrenaline coursed through my veins. My legs trembled with fear and anticipation.

Endless passenger cars snaked by, followed by empty open-bed cargo cars. I followed Ronald's lead exactly, breaking into a run when he did, matching him stride for stride until he signaled me that it was time to jump. Grabbing onto some metal latching, I made a few more strides, then pilled a dive onto the bed of the car.

A second later, Ronald was beside me, laughing.

"Shut up, man! I may not have been a gazelle about it but I got in, didn't I?" I said, socking his shoulder lightly as my fear washed away to relief.

"Yeah, sure, but your head is full of saw dust," he

joked, and the two of us gripped our sides as laughter rolled through us, cleaning out the adrenaline. In a situation where one misstep could have pulled either of us under tons of crushing steel, a little sawdust in the hair was nothing short of fashion. Now, all we had to worry about was avoiding the inspectors.

We found space in the corner of the car to stow our sacks and settled in for the ten-hour ride. The train moved slowly through the city, stopping several times to load more passengers. Some of them made their way back to join us in the cargo cars.

"They paid a reduced fair, but we can't even afford that," Ronald explained. The train finally picked up speed as we pulled out of Kampala, and we dangled our feet off the side of the car, watching the industrial landscape fade into scattered villages, then rolling countryside.

"This is the where the equator crosses Uganda," Ronald said, nudging me to look at a large cement "O" with the word "equator" across its top. "Tourists love to take photos of themselves here."

"So we are right in the middle of the world." I sighed. "I wish I could tell my mother about this adventure."

"What do you mean, Patrick?" Ronald asked, looking over at me with concern. "I thought you said that she gave you the investment money?"

"No. She believes I am going to use the money for school," I said, feeling a hard stab of guilt in my chest.

"That's not good," Ronald said, shaking his head. I felt my face flush in embarrassment, but then he smiled and shrugged. "But hey, you are using the money for school," he amended. "Soon, you will be able to support yourself, even send her money."

My anxiety faded away with his encouragement. We slipped back into silence, as the train weaved through kilometers of dense jungle. Eventually, the trees thinned, then gave way to open savanna. Twilight crept in, and everything became indistinguishable. Ronald and I moved further into the car as the draft created by the moving train began to chill our skin.

"Do these doors ever close?" I asked him, huddling into my thin jacket.

"No, this section was made to carry goods, not passengers," Ronald explained.

"What if a wild animal, say a lion, were to jump through the open doors?"

"I have never heard of that happening," Ronald said, laughing. "But there is always a first time."

Unconcerned, he curled up between his sacks and those of another passenger and immediately started snoring. I sat for a while as the passengers around me fell into hushed whispers, nodding off one by one, until I was the last one awake in the moonlit car. Mild nausea stirred my stomach as the train swayed along, and a rancid odor tickledmy nose. For a while I morbidly entertained myself with guessing its origins—the final assessment being that it was a mixture of a baby's unchanged diaper, body odor, and rotten passion fruit. Finally, my nose and imagination relented, and sleep snatched me away.

*   *   *

I woke up to an orange slice of sun cutting a purple horizon, and the sleepy murmurs of passengers around me.

"Kamwenge, here we come!" Ronald said, stretching his arms gleefully towards the sunrise. The train squealed to a protesting stop.

"C'mon, man! No inspectors, no hassle, and here we are!" he cried, slinging his twine-tied burlaps over his shoulder and making a one-handed vault off the train. With all his energy, I almost thought he'd do a back flip.

"Our luck is holding up so far," I said, following

closely behind.

"They know that the best time to catch entrepreneurs like us is on the way back." Ronald wrinkled his nose. "Then, we'll have merchandise, and we can't run away or afford to abandon it. So, if they catch us they can ticket us, fine us, extract a bribe," he ticked off the risks on his fingers as we walked towards the trading center. My mouth dropped and I pulled to a halt as he continued, "Take possession of all our merchandise and keep it for themselves . . . . Patrick, man, why are you stopped?"

"How can this possibly work?" I exclaimed. Ronald had warned me that we'd have to avoid the inspectors, but this was the first time he'd laid out all the risks so clearly. They scared me.

"Relax, Patrick! C'mon, let's go get some breakfast."

We ate slowly, watching as sun illuminated the rich rolling lands around us. I'd never been to western Uganda, and as I savored my chai tea and pancakes, I took in the new environment. The grass-thatched huts reminded me of home, but there was an unfamiliar cool whip to the air. Heaving, fertile hills surrounded us, the steep land cultivated in uneven terraces to prevent soil erosion during the torrential rains of the wet season. The mountains shone like polished emeralds in the warm light of dawn, so deceivingly close that I wanted to reach out to try to touch them. People moved through the awakening village around us in a slow, happy fashion that eased my anxieties. With full bellies, Ronald and I made our way to the trading center.

Purchasing our produce went smoothly. There were many farmers competing against oneanother, tipping the scales in our favor. When one tried to extract too high a price despite our bargaining, we'd sigh and make as if to visit his neighbor. We ended up with two sacks of Irish potatoes each, as well as half a sack of yellow maize. If everything went well, a profit was in our future.

Because each of our sacks now weighed over a hundred kilos, running with them was not a possibility—we would have to load them before the train started moving. Long before it was scheduled to leave, we hid our goods in some bushes by the tracks. The parked train would hopefully provide enough cover for us to sneak them on board while the inspector concentrated on taking tickets from paying customers.

At 7 p.m., the train warned of its arrival with a blaring horn. As the rusty engine pulled past, passengers exchanged final goodbyes and slung bags on their backs. Some looked poorer and more ragged than we did. Instead of all boarding the passenger cars, a number of them filtered down to line up in front of open-bed cargo cars where we hid. An inspector followed suit to check their tickets, eliciting a string of curses from Ronald.

"Well, there goes our chance to sneak on board.

We'll have to try to pay him off," Ronald said.

"Can we still make a profit if we do that?"

"Oh, we won't be paying full fare. This is just a bribe so we can get our goods on the train. Don't worry," he added with a sarcastic smirk, "It won't guarantee us any security."

While Ronald negotiated with the inspector, I hid in the bushes so we'd only have to pay for one of us and our goods. Everything went smoothly, and Ronald paid a young boy a few pennies to help him load our sacs. The boy struggled under the weight, and the process went too slowly. As they pushed at the third bag, the train began to move.

In a second, I jumped from the bushes and swung onto the moving car, grabbing hold of the sack and hefting it onto the bed.

"Hurry, hand me the sacks!" I hissed.

He and the boy raced to grab the rest of the sacks as

the train slowly gained momentum. I yanked the bags out of their hands with ferocity that would leave me sore for days after—though in that moment I didn't feel a thing.

The final half-sack was the lightest, but by the time Ronald got to it, the train was picking up speed and his legs were tired. He matched the locomotive's pace but couldn't spare any energy to lift the sack within my reach.

"Ronald, leave the goods and get on the train!" I begged, holding my hand out for him to grab.

But he shook his head, and I could tell by the set of his sweat-streaked face that he wasn't giving up on that corn.

"Hey!" he called over to some men who sat at a bar alongside the tracks. They shouted cheers to our slow-speed race and toasted with their beers. "Come help! Patrick," he wheezed, "Throw them some shillings!"

As I fumbled in my pockets for the cash, the farmers put down their drinks, and with slightly-drunk enthusiasm raced to catch up with Ronald. They took the sack from his tired hands and tossed it on the train as I pulled my friend on board. Paying not a bit of attention to the money that I offered them, they waved after us and yelled words of good luck instead.

*   *   *

Ronald and I found a spot in the corner of the car and stacked our goods around us as protection from the cold. As night set in, passengers around us pulled out bottles of hard liquor to warm themselves from the inside. We munched on dry biscuits and sipped from metal flasks of cold water. I thought about what a luxury our icy drinks would be in the heat of Kampala. Here, they were anything but.

At midnight a tall, dark man walked into our car, flanked by two large muscular companions. They looked ominous. I nudged Ronald.

"That's the inspector with his enforcement guards," he whispered, stiffening. "Quick, let's pretend we are going to use the toilet in the passenger car. Don't look at them when you walk past."

Ronald stood up and sauntered quietly down towards the inspectors. When he'd made it half-way down the car, I followed casually in his path. I hesitated until the inspector and his men were engaged in asking a pretty young woman carrying several bushels of bananas for her ticket, then brushed past.

Just through the door, in the swaying space between cars, Ronald stopped to peek through the small window. I joined him, watching with apprehension as the inspectors neared our baggage.

"Oh, man! We should have hid it better. I bet we could have squeezed at least two sacks under that sugarcane," Ronald lamented. We watched as the inspectors pointed at our goods and began questioning the people nearest to them. Ronald squeezed his eyes closed and banged his head quietly on the wall.

"Wait," I shook his shoulder. "He just walked away from our bags."

Ronald pushed me out of the little window to look. "Huh. You're right."

We stood for a minute, watching dumbfounded, then went to hide in the toilet until we were sure the inspectors had completed their rounds and made their way back up through the cars.

When we finally returned to our car, we asked the old man stationed next to us what had happened. He pointed to a small woman sitting in the corner, wrapped in layers of thick earth-tone scarves. "She claimed your packages as her own," he said.

*   *   *

I sat up late that night, contemplating the kindness of this stranger. She'd humbly accepted our thanks, and waved off any offer of monetary compensation as if it was an insult. I recalled the drunken farmers, who had helped us load our final bag with fun-loving generosity. They too had refused compensation, but they'd also clearly enjoyed the thrill, and it was their village our purchase supported. But why had this woman put herself at risk to help us?

Early the next morning, the train made an extra-long stop so that people could get out, stretch, and purchase refreshments. The kind woman gathered up her things and disembarked. I followed after.

"Excuse me miss," I said, falling into step alongside of her. "I am the one you helped by claiming those bags of potatoes as your own."

"Yes, I recognize you," she answered with a smile. She paused at a kiosk to purchase a warm cup of coffee with milk. I stood by and waited for her. "Would you like anything?" she asked.

"Not to eat, thank you," I replied. "But I would like to know - why did you do it?"

She turned to me, and for the first time I could study her face. She was in her early twenties, and beneath the scarves she was quite beautiful, though there was a certain sadness to her large brown eyes. "Since you are so curious, I will tell you my story. I helped you because I overheard you talk about school on the train. I have seen your struggle, and I know that you are doing this because you have to - not because you want to. It makes me sad that our world is this way. But you are hard-working boys, and smart, and if you continue to persevere, you will not be forced to do this forever.

"I once dreamed of an education and a career, but after I became pregnant at an early age, my father disowned me. The father of my child offered no support; I left him because he abused me. I was forced to drop out before I'd even finished lower secondary. For years I sought a way to go back to school, but no one was there, no one came to my rescue. Now, I spend my life trading potatoes." The woman's voice softened. She wiped her eyes with a handkerchief, stealing a glance at the train as it blew its warning whistle. "Don't ever give up. Ignorant people can take many things from you, but not your dreams."

Fifteen

January 1992 *(Kampala, Uganda)*

Agatare*(market)*

Like ants competing for sugar crumbs, retailers at the
Kampala marketplace swarmed our potato stand. Selling
the produce turned out to be as easy as purchasing it.
Collecting payment, on the other hand, was far more
difficult than we'd anticipated. As was normal at the
market, we allowed buyers to pay only a portion of the
negotiated price up front, leaving us with promises for
future payment of the balance. A few made good on their
word, but our youth and inexperience made us an easy

target for swindle. Though we didn't make as much profit as we'd anticipated, my share was still enough to pay for a third of a year's school tuition. We managed four more trading trips before the school year started. The box under my bed slowly filled, and by the first day of school it contained just enough cash to cover a year's tuition. I'd have nothing left over to invest, but at least I'd bought myself one more year of schooling.

*   *   *

On a short break between trading trips, I made the walk to Kampala High to pick up my exit exam scores and--if I'd passed--my certificate of completing of lower secondary school. The day was blistering and my mind clouded with thoughts of how bleak life would be if my brief foray into sports and girls cost me my education. I imagined myself stooped over with age, deep lines in my face, still riding the trains with sacks of potatoes.

When I arrived, Mr. Zubair, the chemistry teacher, stood solitary guard over the school's wrought iron gates. I advised him of my purpose and he allowed me inside, then locked the entrance solemnly behind us and led the way towards the registrar's office.

"The registrar is out of the office, so I'm covering his duties," he explained.

"Are you in charge of everything here?" I joked, as he flipped through a huge ring of keys to unlock the door.

He answered with a wry smile. It looked surprising on his usually stern face. Inside the office, he pulled open an old filing cabinet and flipped through to find my name. "Kalenzi. Here you are--your certificate. You passed, but not by much, young man." He raised a bushy eyebrow at me.

"What would you advise me to do with these scores?" I asked, gripping the certificate tightly to my chest.

"Let me look at this again." He gently inched the paper from my hands. "Well, it appears you are better in science than you are in arts. I recommend you take physics, chemistry, biology and sub-mathematics as a combination."

I thanked him for his advice, then dawdled near the gardens while he walked back to the gate to admit another student. I knew Mr. Zubair's reputation as a strict and uncompromising disciplinarian. Most of the students resented his firm ways, but I wished the school had more teachers like him. Sure, he didn't coddle students, but he was perhaps the only one I'd encountered at Kampala High who seemed to truly care that the school deliver a quality education. I wanted to talk to him more, but worried about taking up his time. I wasn't sure what to do or say. Luckily, he saved me the effort.

"Most of those students passed with a C score," he confided, strolling over to sit beside me on a moss-streaked rock veranda. "Many of them lack desire or ability to do better. But," he gave me a stern look, "you are different. Sure, last year, you played around and chose your friends poorly. That has to change. However--," he fixed me with a hard gaze and gestured towards the gate. "If you work hard for the next two years, you stand a better chance than any of them to get into university."

"But I need to do more than get into the university!" the frustrated words burst out of me. "I need to be one of the top three thousand highest-scoring students in the whole country to earn a full scholarship! Otherwise, it is pointless—there is no way I can afford to pay."

"Patrick, don't let these worries get to you," Mr. Zubair said in a soft tone. He nodded towards the gate. "I can tell you are ashamed of your past. You are jealous of that boy whose parents drove him away in a nice car, aren't you?"

"What are you, a psychic?" I joked, blushing.

He laughed and gave a shrug, but his voice took on a low, serious tone. "I have been in your situation. Don't ever let your past define you. It is who you think you are, and who you want to be, that determines your fate. Don't give up on your dreams, Patrick."

*   *   *

For the next year, I threw myself relentlessly into my schoolwork. I quit boxing, going to the movies, hanging out with girls—all the activities that could serve as distractions. Even as I watched my peers merrily engaging in those teenage pastimes, I no longer felt a sense of jealousy. I was consumed with desire to excel at my A-level exams and earn a scholarship to Makerere University.

The odds were not stacked in my favor. First, I was competing with nearly a hundred thousand students across the country for only a few thousand spots. Many of them attended boarding schools, had high-quality teaching, participatory classmates and easy access to labs, libraries, and other resources--an environment designed to maximize their potential. While they could roll out of their bunks and into class, I had to spend hours each day just making the three-mile walk to school and back. Then there was Kampala High. It didn't fail to live up to its reputation as the city's worst school. I knew that few of its graduates gained enrollment in the university, let alone earn a scholarship. I'd made several attempts to enroll at a better school, but even with family connections my poor O-level grades were an insurmountable roadblock. Kampala High was my only option, and I had to make the best of it. Mr. Zubair took on the role of mentor and ally, pushing me relentlessly. I studied all the way through every break, leaving time for neither work nor family. When I finally went home for Christmas at the end of my first year, it was, again, with empty pockets.

*   *   *

I found Dada sitting under his mulberry tree smoking a pipe. He looked even paler and thinner than he had last year, and his eyes had a sickly yellow hue. When he hugged me, there was no strength to his grip.

"How are you are doing?" I asked, pulling an old wooden bench over to sit beside him.

"Not so well," he admitted. "The burdens of taking care of a large family are catching up with me. I haven't been in the best health."

I asked if he'd seen a doctor, but he assured me that he'd be better soon, and that it was my aging grandpa I should be worrying about. As we were catching up, my mother and siblings came out of the house with big smiles and warm greetings. My mother looked healthy and strong as ever, though worry lines spread from the corners of her eyes and deepened sadly when I asked her why there were

417

only six children. She'd had to send Grace away to be cared for by her mother in Buruli. I didn't have to ask if it was because of our dwindling finances.

As soon as the excitement died down enough that I could escape from the clinging arms of my siblings, I made my way over to Baaba's house, where I found him napping in his hammock. Though his eyesight no longer allowed him to clearly make out my face, his grip was still strong-- stronger than that of my father.

As we sat talking, the subject of my school fees came up. I filled Baaba in on my potato-selling business and my journeys to Western Uganda. "But I don't have the funds nor the time to do that again this year," I added sadly. "I'm just hoping for a miracle."

"Go and rest," Baaba said, arranging himself to a more comfortable position, thebright strands of the hammock squeaking beneath him. "We will discuss this matter with your parents tomorrow."

                    *   *   *

The next morning, Mama, Dada and I walked over to
Baaba's. He was sitting in his chair, gazing off into the
distance. His head lifted at the sound of us drawing near.

"There you are, town boy." he said to me with a
smile that wrinkled his cloudy eyes.

"I will never be a town boy. I will be a herdsman
for life!" I laughed.

"Oh really?" Dada said, smiling and elbowing me
gently. "Can you still tolerate heavy rain and long hours in
the wilderness?"

"Of course I can," I assured him, puffing out my
chest.

"Okay you two," Mama said, pointing at me and
Dada. "You must be civil in this discussion. Let's get
started. I have a lot to do today."

Dada and I pulled up a bench, and we all settled

down, facing Baaba.

There was a moment of respectful silence as Grandpa tapped his pipe. With an authoritative clearing of his throat, he began: "We need to figure out how Patrick is going to pay for his school fees."

"Father," Dada immediately interjected, shaking his head, "There is nothing to figure out. We are worse off than we were this time last year." He clapped his hands to his thighs as if to declare the conversation over.

Baaba and Mama immediately shifted their eyes to me, anticipating a reaction. I raised my palms.

"I promise I will not argue or talk back this time. I just want to finish school."

"Patrick," Mama said, a pained expression wrinkling her brow. "Your father is right; we have nothing left to give you."

Silence stole over the moment. Baaba leaned in towards Mama and Dada. Resting his elbows on his knees, he peered at them with an intensity that eclipsed his unseeing eyes.

"You both know that Rwabagabo is not going to quit, right?" he said. "If you deny him, you will just drive him to dubious means. I understand that you don't have any more money to give, but I also watch you waste it every day." He stared directly in my father's eyes. "From the looks of things, the way this family is going, Patrick will be the redeemer of your future. I will be long gone but you . . . you will be here without anything if you do not hang onto this hope." He gently tapped my knee with his arthritic finger. "So, what are you going to do?"

Mama and Dada exchanged looks like guilty children.

"Maybe I can sell one cow," Dada finally said, the words pushing painfully from his mouth. "But that will only pay for one term. And it will leave me with only two cows—there is no way I can sell any more without starving my family."

Gratitude filled me. I knew that giving up that cow would mean a serious dent in my father's ability to purchase liquor—it was a big sacrifice for him. I wanted to hug him, but kept trembling to my chair, waiting for the commitment to be finalized.

"John, since you are willing to make this investment in your son's education, I will make one as well," Baaba said.

Dada looked at him quizzically, and I felt the breath catch in my throat. "I need you to ask the local chief to come out tomorrow and adjust a few things in my will. I guarantee that my grandson's last year of high school will be paid for by me, dead or alive."

"Over the years, I have given each of my sons a wife and allotted them a herd," he continued. "I have given my daughters enough too, and I don't need much to live on. So, Rwabagabo, you will receive my inheritance. It is not much, but with God's grace, it may help you on your path to achieving what no one in this family ever has—a university education. My life is ending and yours is just beginning."

* * *

The sacrifices that my family was making to invest in my education fueled and focused me like nothing ever had. Earning admittance and full scholarship to Makerere was no longer a wistful dream—it was something I had to achieve. I could not let my family down. Not only must my class grades be perfect, but my test scores must be as well. I studied obsessively.

This wasn't easy. At Uncle Yosia's, there was no privacy. I shared a room with several of my cousins, and all the little children running about made merely keeping track of my school materials difficult. Focusing on them was a whole other challenge. I was constantly on the lookout for a better place to study.

On my walks to and from school, I noticed a neighboring house that was almost always empty. One day, in desperation and with the shouts of my cousins echoing in my head, I walked right up to its high fence and called over to the groundskeeper. When he came over to see what I wanted, my life story came out in a torrent. He listened with rapt attention, and when I asked if there was any way I could study in the house while the owner was away, he agreed to help me.

I spent as much time as I could in that lonely mansion, lost in my school books. It was alien and quiet, with stark furnishing, high ceilings, and thick walls that made for an ideal study environment. When I needed a break, I'd stroll through the rolling lawns and garden, looking out on the city spread below.

One glistening afternoon, when I was out taking a

break from a difficult physics problem, I saw a girl walking along the path that looped behind the house. She was wearing a school uniform and carried a heavy backpack. She flashed me a captivating smile as she passed.

"Hi," I daringly greeted her.

"Hi," she answered, turning to cast a quick look without slowing her gait.

"Wait!" I called, and jogged to catch up. I walked on my side of the fence, matching her pace.

She pulled to a stop and turned to face me, but kept her eyes down. With the tip of her shoe, she traced a circle in the dirt.

"What's your name?" I asked, pressing my face to the fence.

"I'm Sharon," she replied, finally meeting my eyes. A brief but welcoming grin flashed across her face. "What's yours?"

"Patrick," I answered. "Where do you live?"

"That way, about ten houses up the street." She pointed, but I was too fixated on her beautifully curved lips, her chocolate skin, and her perfect dimples to let my gaze leave her.

"I haven't seen you here before. Did you just move in?" she asked. A smile crept across her face, no doubt due to the moonstruck look on my face. Her crescent-shaped eyes were an intoxicating shade of brown, and thick black lashes framed them like lace.

"No, I don't live here," I managed, blinking to regain my composure. That she thought this could be my house caused me to chuckle.

"What's so funny?" she asked.

"I only come here to read books . . . . Where I live is nothing like this," I said, smiling and shaking my head as I pointed to the house behind me.

"You're funny . . . what does it matter?" She giggled and turned back in the direction she was headed. "It was nice talking to you--Patrick, right?"

I nodded, following alongside her as she began walking again. "It was nice talking to you too." The fence turned and I could no longer follow. "Will you pass by here tomorrow?" I called after her.

"I'm not sure." She replied, spinning around and walking backwards to give me one more look at those deadly eyes. "But I take this path a lot, so . . . maybe I will see you again." She flashed a final smile, and I stood staring after the woman who would someday be my wife until she disappeared up the tree-lined path.

*　　　*　　　*

"What will you study at the university, Rwabagabo?" Baaba asked, as we strolled the perimeter of his *kraal*.

"I haven't been accepted yet, Baaba,"

"Oh, I have no doubt you will make it in."

The last year of school had passed by in a blink. I'd done nothing but study. Even after meeting Sharon, I'd been only further motivated to spend as much time as I could with my nose in my books—especially when it meant studying on the lawn that she passed by every day. We'd developed a friendly routine and, after our brief conversations, my whole world was recharged. Answers to the most difficult math problems coalesced in my head, paragraphs rolled from my pen; everything seemed clear. When time finally came to take the pivotal A-level exit exams that would determine whether I earned scholarship to Makerere, I completed them with calm confidence. Afterward, I caught a bus home to visit with my family and weather the painful waiting period until I knew whether I'd made the cut-off.

*　　*　　*

"Well, if I get in, I'll probably study science. I could be a pharmacist, an engineer, an architect. Maybe a doctor or an

agriculturalist."

"With this science thing," Baaba said, tugging on

the fence to check its sturdiness, "can you study something

that I could understand in my old and uneducated ways?"

"Like what, Baaba?"

"Well," he stopped and turned to face me, "our

tradition and way of life is defined by cattle. We are part of

a farming tribe. So, could you learn to treat animals, like

the doctor who comes here to heal our cows and dogs? The

work would fit your upbringing and heritage, and it appears

to pay well, too."

"You wish for me to be a veterinarian?" I asked.

"Yes, if you think you might like it," Baaba said.

"There is no greater life than being paid to do something

you enjoy."

I mulled over the idea for a minute, looking out at

the cattle, thinking of how much I'd always loved the

animals I grew up alongside. "I think I would love it!" I declared, putting a big smile on my grandfather's face.

"Good man, my Rwabagabo," He said. "Now, the next thing will be to find you a beautiful young woman to start a family with. I would like to see my great grandchildren before I die." He gave me a keen smile.

"First school, then family," I said, and we both laughed.

"I don't want an arranged marriage," I added.

"Why? I think that the marriages in our family have been successful."

"True, but I'm different. I want to marry someone I have gotten to know and chosen myself."

"Is there anyone you have in mind, Rwabagabo?" Baaba asked, giving me a suspicious sideward gaze.

I thought about Sharon. "Not that I'm anywhere close to marrying, but I have met a girl. If things work out, I can see myself being with her for a long time."

Sixteen

January 1993 *(Kampala, Uganda)*

News *(amakuru)*

I returned to Kampala the night before the admittance results were to be published at Makerere University. Sleep came to me only in anxiety-filled fits, and before the sun had risen I couldn't stand waiting longer and made my way down to the university. I forced my restless legs to move slowly, knowing that it was unlikely the gates would be open so early. My heart thudded so heavily in my chest I feared it would explode, and I glanced at work-bound passersby to see if they too could hear it. The few who met my gaze must have read the mask of anxiety on my face, for they flashed faint smiles of comfort.

To my surprise, the university gates stood open when I arrived. The sun, just risen, sparkled on the dewy lawns. When I arrived at the announcement board outside the admissions office, a few students were already there, tracing the tiny print of long white lists with their fingers. I fidgeted impatiently while they scrolled through with a slowness that seemed impossible for a college hopeful. Finally, I was alone with the board. My vision clouded. Black lines faded into each other. My finger shook as I held it to the paper, tracing down through the Hs, the Js ... then, I saw my name. Kalenzi. I'd been admitted to veterinary medicine and awarded the government scholarship.

I stood for a moment, unable to process the reality of my lifelong dream. Then, in a torrent, it hit me. "Yes!" I hollered into the crisp morning air. "This is for Baaba!"

The prospective students waiting behind me smiled and shuffled, and a professor passing by gave me a thumbs-up. I wanted to hug each and every one of them. I wished

for a time machine to transport me home so I could tell

Baaba and my parents that their sacrifices had not been in

vain—that I'd done this for them. But celebrating with

Baaba would have to wait until the end of the semester.

Instead, I stole one final look at my starred name, just to

make sure it was real and to cement the image in my mind.

Then I took off running back towards Uncle Yosia's. He

too had made this possible, and I couldn't wait to share the

a makuru, news. Plus, classes would start in a week, and it

was time to get ready.

*   *   *

It was in the simple dormitories of Makerere that I

experienced for the first time the luxuries of electricity and

running water. Between these conveniences, the free board,

the quiet study areas, and the fact that I no longer had to

spend hours every day just walking to school, my academic proficiency soared. As classes breezed by, all the worries that I'd carried into Makerere faded. Concerns that my meager education at one of the country's worst schools would leave me ill-prepared for the rigors of university were laid to rest by the end of my first week. By the second week, I had adjusted well to the rich multi-cultural environment with wealthy students coming from high-profile boarding schools across Uganda and abroad. Soon, I walked the campus with a confidence firmly rooted in my easy acclimation to the rigors of academia—a place where, more than anywhere before in my life, I was treated as an equal, without discrimination or bias.

I had enrolled in the University's school of veterinary medicine, where I found that my childhood of herding, milking, protecting and living with cattle and other animals gave me an unexpected comfort in the rigorous veterinary medicine course. On the occasions when I had an opportunity to travel home during breaks, Baaba and I discussed my studies in anatomy and pathology in layman's terms that allowed easy surmounting of our educational division. I valued the traditional knowledge that he continued to imbue me with, as he enjoyed the new information that I brought to him. Though he was no longer actively caring for cattle, he still served as advisor for many. He valued gaining new knowledge and would continue to until his death.

*   *   *

Four years flew by without incident except for worrisome news that came from home. My family struggled with the increasing cost of renting land. The four cows they used for milk were barely producing milk for the large family. As I neared graduation with a score that placed me firmly in the top of my class, it seemed that nothing could slow my fast-track to a flourishing career capable of sustaining my parents, Baaba, and perhaps a family of my own.

My relationship with Sharon continued to grow like the mulberry tree in my family's backyard, protective and nourishing, deeply rooted in mutual respect, trust, and a love that grew stronger every time we saw each other. Sharon still studied in a private boarding school. When we could sneak away from classes together, we spent hours sculpting the life we'd create together; a big beautiful house, children, my own veterinary practice, and enough income that I could raise my family from their perpetual poverty.

Then, on the morning of September 14, 1996, two months before my graduation, the realities of life came crashing back down upon my proud shoulders. Mid-way through a pharmacology lecture, a laboratory assistant came hurrying into the classroom and whispered in my professor's ear, cutting him off abruptly. Eyes slowly rose from notes as the class looked to see what was going on. The professor met my eye, and with a solemn face motioned me forward. "Patrick, you have a guest waiting outside. He says it's very important."

There were only a few people who would come visit me at the university. I couldn't imagine any of them having cause to pull me out of class. A ball of fear grew in my stomach as I hurriedly gathered my things and rushed out of the classroom.

My cousin Fred, who lived near my family in Baale, waited outside, pacing anxiously. I opened my mouth to greet him, but the pained expression on his face made the words catch in my throat. I knew something was wrong.

For a long pause, neither of us spoke. Finally, I was able to force a dry swallow. "Fred, is there a problem at home?" I asked.

"Yes, I—" His eyes searched the sky above my head and he folded his arms over his chest as if he were cold. I waited in the cool wash of silence. Finally, he said, "Your father died last night."

My legs weakened, grief and confusion washed over me. "You mean my grandfather?" I asked. I'd long dreaded and anticipated my aging grandfather's death; in a way I was prepared for it to be announced in a moment like this. But the thought of my father's mortality had not occurred to me. I was sure that through his grief, Fred must have misspoken.

"No, your father, John Kafuniza. I'm sorry, cousin. He passed last night."

Fred and I remained silent for a few more moments. I kept my tear-filled eyes up towards the sky, while my mind rewound time, flipping through a lifetime of memories, imprinted like snapshots in my mind.

*   *   *

I caught the next bus to Baale, and arrived home to a house whose walls shook with wailing.

Before I reached the veranda, my sister Annet came running and fell into my arms, her face stained and swollen with sorrow. "Patrick, my dear brother, Dada is gone! He is gone!" she cried. I hugged her close, offering what comfort I could, and trying to hold back my own tears by keeping my gaze moving over the familiar landscape of our home. Then, my eyes rested on the old mulberry tree where Dada and I had passed so many sunny afternoons. I held my sister and cried.

Baaba sat with my uncles and a few other men under the tree, his gaze somewhere none of us could see. Removingmyself from my sister's embrace, I tried to regain my composure and walked over to join them.

"Rwabagabo," Baaba greeted, seeming to recognize me from my footsteps. "I am terribly sorry about your father."

"I am sorry about your son," I replied.

"It is horrible to be as old as I am and have to bury my fifty-two-year-old son," Baaba said. His voice grated with age and pain, but there was still a strand of strength in the way he sat. "Now go see your mother. She is by her husband's body."

I followed the sound of my mother's crying into the house to where she sat beside the still body, covered with a white sheet and laid out on the mattress they had shared every night of their married life. A candle flickered softly at the head of the bed.

"Son, thank God you're home!" Mama cried when she saw me. She pushed herself up and drew me to her breast. Her voice was hoarse from hours of crying and her hands gripped tightly around my shoulders as if beyond her control.

"I'm sorry. I wish I would have been with you when he passed," I said, stilling myself with deep breaths.

"You couldn't have changed his destiny. God needs him more than we do. But come close and see him for the last time," my mother replied. She pulled the white sheet off his face.

There was calmness to his expression, and I could almost believe that he's just had one too many drinks and fallen asleep. But then—his body, much smaller than I ever recalled, seemed impossibly cold and still.

I reset the sheet, and sat next to Mama, staring off into space as my mind wrestled with this new reality.

Like grandpa, I would acknowledge but control my sorrow. I must stay strong, for my mother, for my sisters—for every person in my family who, with my father's death, would now look to me as the head of the household.

"Where is the rest of the family?" I asked, nodding as my mother haltingly ticked off their various whereabouts.

"When will we bury him?"

"Definitely tomorrow, before his body begins to disintegrate into a dishonorable form," she said. "Don't you agree?"

"Of course, Mama. Can you tell me how he died?"

Mama cleared her throat and wiped at her tear stained cheeks with the back of her hand. "It was bizarre and sudden," she began. "He complained of not feeling well four days ago, but went about his chores. Yesterday afternoon--as Annet and I were inside cleaning—we heard a horrible sound from outside. It will never leave my ears. I can't describe it, but it was as though he was agonizing in pain and trying to call for someone at the same time. Something like a choked out scream."

"Annet and I rushed outside. We found your father on the ground beneath the mulberry tree. He'd fallen off his chair and was on the ground, struggling with unseen demons. I held him in my lap and I told Annet to call Uncle Kafuuko. As soon as Kafuuko and Annet arrived, your father . . . called out Annet's name and . . . took his last breath." Mama choked out the last words, fresh tears welling at the corners of her eyes.

I couldn't stop my medically-trained brain from analyzing the cause of my father's death. Under my querying, my mother divulged that in his last months, he'd complained of headaches, painful joints, swollen feet, and losing weight.

"Did he go to the hospital?" I asked.

"Ha! You know your father. No matter how we urged him to, he insisted he would be fine. He refused."

I spun the symptoms through my head. It seemed likely that liver disease or a heart attack had taken Dada's life; that alcohol had played a role was clear. I gave my mother my assessment, the closest thing to a postmortem that my father would receive.

"I guess we will never know," she said, and turned aside to once again fill her hands with tears.

*　　*　　*

I stayed with my family for the next three days and nights, as was Tutsi custom. During that time, friends, relatives, and neighbors all gathered at our house, bringing food, companionship, songs, and tears. At night, we lit huge bonfires; by day, chores were quickly done with so many hands. Baaba and I had time to sit and discuss school; he worried about my being distracted from studying so close to finals, but I assured him that I could spare the time.

What we didn't discuss yet was who would care for the family now that father was gone. Though he drank away most of our resources before he died, my father had still tended the cows, kept food in the kitchen, and been a pillar of strength for all of us. Now that he was gone, I worried the family would begin to crumble. I knew that it was nearly time for me assume my position as provider. What I didn't know is how I would balance that with the rest of my dreams—of finishing school, of having my own family, of practicing the profession I'd invested many years in.

When the roosters crowed daybreak on our second day of mourning, I set out with three of my uncles to dig father's grave. We picked a spot just north of the house, where he could still look out over the cattle and our family. The dirt pulled heavy from the earth, and the yawning void it left looked too deep, too dark. I couldn't bear the thought of my father laid to rest down there, covered up and locked forever in a wooden box, but there was nothing to be done. I knew that someday I'd find my final rest in a place not so different.

By two o'clock, the freshly dug earth had begun to crust, and a hundred mourners filled our yard. The crowd parted, then closed in behind like a sea, as I led our family and the four men bearing Dada's coffin to the grave. A priest prayed over his body in the sobbing grief, a soft lilt of praise that brought a drizzle down from the pregnant sky. It was as if our land too cried for my father, who had spent his days wandering these forests with his cattle in search of pasture, water, or just a good shaded tree to lean against while he carved a stick and looked out over his herd and the rolling savannah. The mourners bade their private goodbyes and slowly faded back towards the house. My uncles and I tossed the heavy earth over the simple wooden box, back into the hole we'd just dug. When the last shovelful had been thrown, they too left, and I was alone with my father. I lay one final stone over his grave, then knelt before it, my knees digging into the soft earth.

John, Father, my Dada . . . I promise you, I will always be a good man, a responsible father and son. I will take care of our Baaba, of Mama, of all your children; I will take care of all their children. I will work my whole life to make you proud. Oh Dada--I will miss you so much. 'Til we meet again . . .

*   *   *

When the period of mourning drew to an end, I reluctantly bid leave of my family to return to Makerere for my last weeks of school. As much as it hurt me to leave them there, sick with grief and with neither provider nor protector, I'd come to the firm conclusion--one supported by Baaba--that the way I could ultimately help most was by finishing my degree and finding a job. That didn't make parting any easier.

"What are we going to do, Patrick?" Annet asked, as I stood at the doorway, unable to turn my back on the circle of wide-eyed children crowded around me like hatchlings awaiting food from a mother bird. My mouth worked wordlessly as I struggled to find an answer for her, to soothe the doubt and confusion in the silent faces that held me.

Annet took another step forward, reaching out to grab my wrist. Tears welled in her eyes. "Who is going to take care of us?"

I felt my suitcase grow unbearably heavy in my hand as the burden of choice and responsibility fell cripplingly upon my shoulders. As if reading my struggle, mother stepped between us.

"Don't burden him, children," she said, softly taking Annet's hand from my wrist. "He needs to concentrate on his final months at the university."

"Family is never a burden, Mama," I said, giving her a gentle smile of thanks. "Do you have enough food for the next few months?"

"Don't worry about us, son," she insisted. "Concentrate on your finals. Your education may be the ultimate savior for this family."

Igitaramo *(celebration)*

Two months later, the sorrow and grieving brought on by

my father's death was replaced by celebration as I became the first member of our family to earn a university degree. The whole family made the trek from Baale to watch me walk down the aisle and receive my degree from the hands of our country's president, Yoweri Museveni, the man who had led NRA rebel fighters to save the country from a military regime. Even Baaba insisted on making the voyage, despite the discomfort of those tightly-packed commuter busses with their poor suspension and stifling heat.

"He said he would rather die traveling than miss your graduation," Mama explained when I asked why she hadn't convinced him to stay home.

At the ceremony, my mother, surrounded by a flock of children and wearing a pair of shiny borrowed shoes, cheered above all the rest as the president announced our graduation. Looking out at her elegant figure, a brilliant and bold flash of color in the crowd, long arms outstretched as her clapping rang with pride and joy, I was transported back to a similar moment, endless years ago, when I'd won a poetry reading contest at Mr. Rueben's village school.

We partied until the small hours of the morning in a rented ballroom, eating, drinking, and dancing ourselves into grateful exhaustion. Amid the festivities, Baaba expressed his winking approval of Sharon and her family, there to share the celebration, Uncle Yosia and Edith glowed in pride as if I were their son. Baaba always called me Rwabagabo, a fighter, but I knew it was the love and support of the people who surrounded me, along with that of my father, whose spirit I felt smiling down, who had made this possible. They had made so many selfless sacrifices to help me make it this far. Now, it was time for me to turn around and take care of them.

Seventeen

February, 1999 *(Kampala)*

Ubworo *(poverty)*

For several months after I graduated, I worked to earn
income by patching together small jobs from pet owners
and farmers who heard about me through word of mouth.
Though this brought in enough money to feed my family
and rent a room in one of the worst slums on the edge of
Kampala, I saw quickly that it wasn't a means of achieving
the career I desired for myself, nor the stability I desired for
my family. I tried a salaried position at a dairy farm, but the
pay there was even more dismal. I found myself fighting a
gnawing worry that my education would not be enough to
pull my family from *Ubworo*, poverty. I worked

relentlessly, bought myself no luxuries, and yet was struggling just to keep my siblings in school. My idea was that, at this point, I'd be saving to buy homes for my mother and, eventually, Sharon and myself. It now seemed a bad-humored joke. I'd just submitted an application for yet another avenue of employment—working with a government-funded program to improve animal husbandry in rural counties—when I received a letter from my mother.

Dear son,

We have missed you since you graduated. I am very proud of you, and pray that your endeavors will always be blessed by God.

Things are not going well here. The landlord wants us off of the property in a week. I asked your half-brother, John, if we could move onto his land. If you remember, his land is a hundred and twenty kilometers from our house. We are planning to move as soon as you can find us money to hire a truck to move our things and the four cows we have left. John shares the land with his father's children, so we will not be able to stay there very long, but we hope God will open up another window for us soon.

Thank you for the money and the food packages you have been sending us; they have kept us alive and the kids are able to go to school.

My heart is broken because Baaba can't move with us; Uncle Kafuuko will keep him. But, if you remember,Kafuuko drinks a lot and doesn't take good care of grandpa. He and his family also have to vacate their land. They will be relocating to a forest reserve nearby. I wish it could be different but there is nothing I can do.

As soon as you find any money, please send it or come and get us out of here.

Your mother,

Florence Kafuniza

Crumpling the paper in my hands, I collapsed onto my mattress. Above me, water stained the ceiling, threatening rot. The walls of my bedroom seemed a metaphor for my life: dark, ugly, and uneven. That night, I tossed and turned in my bed waiting for sleep, but all I could think of was my mother and siblings, waiting under a roof that was no longer theirs; of old Baaba, hiding in the jungle with only my drunken uncle to care for him; of my family, chased from their home yet again.

*   *   *

Relief filled me briefly when I was offered the animal husbandry job days later, but it was soon to fade away. While this position had promised all the lucrative stability and benefits of a titled government position, it delivered something quite different. Corruption was so deeply engrained in the system that I couldn't move an inch without some official taking a dime from my pocket. For every livestock transportation permit I signed and got paid for, a local chief demanded a kickback; for every cow I inspected, a portion of my fee went into a bureaucrat's pocket. The district cashiers, whose responsibility it was to distribute my salary, consistently skimmed a bit off the top for themselves, and not even the motorcycles promised us for transportation to the distant rural farms we serviced ever showed up. I made my rounds on a rickety old rented bicycle, lived in a squalid room, and watched helplessly as both my income and my budget for serving this community were diminished by greed.

I'd been working this lonely job for four months when Sharon came to pay me a surprise visit. The remote village was hours from Kampala, and I was both touched and a little embarrassed to arrive home from work at 9 pm and find her sitting on the rough mattress that served as both bed, chair and sofa in my meager accommodations.

"Hey, where have you been?" she asked as she got up to hug me. "I've been waiting here for four hours. I was worried about you."

"Welcome to Kamira," I said with a half-smile. As I took her by the elbow and guided her out of my empty apartment to our village's lone restaurant, I related the story of my evening; my old bike broke down on the way back from a farm ten kilometers away, and I had to walk home. It was, unfortunately, nothing new.

We sat down at a plastic table where a bleary-eyed waitress brought us two dishes of Matooke and stew. The stew was congealed, and the plantains were cold and tough. Sharon took one bite, swallowed with a grimace, and then pushed the plate aside.

"You don't like the food?" I asked.

She shook her head. In a tender voice, she asked, "How long are you going to live like this?"

I studied the plate in front of me, as if I could find the answer in the cold chunks of matooke. "Not much longer," I told her. "I can't do this much longer. My family is homeless; I can barely keep skin on their bones and afford school fees, let alone think of buying them land. You see where I live—my possessions are beyond meager—I am lucky that the toothbrush I use is mine, and not borrowed."

"So, what will you do?"

"I have tried everything in this country. There is no escaping the corruption here--it runs too deep. I spend my time dealing with bureaucratic messes and implementing ill-planned government programs rather than actually practicing medicine. I don't see how I can ever do the kind of work I am capable of here, let alone be paid what I deserve." The words came rolling off me like a heavy load, and as they lifted, an idea that had been simmering beneath my consciousness for months finally surfaced.

"I'm considering leaving Uganda." As the words left my mouth I could already feel the sting they would cause, and I turned my face away quickly so as not to see the hurt in her eyes.

She reached out, took hold of my chin and turned my face to look her straight in the eyes."Are you being serious?"

"Sharon—I am in a desperate situation. Yes."

Suddenly, the little restaurant was stifling hot; I couldn't breathe. I pushed myself up from the table and went outside to fill my lungs with the fresh air. When I returned, Sharon's face shone with tears.

"Where are you going to go?" she asked hoarsely.

"I don't know--overseas--"

"How will you even get the money?" she interrupted.

"I don't know yet."

The pain in her eyes deepened and her voice hardened. "What about us, Patrick?"

"I—I don't know."

Sharon leaned in, grasping my hand so fiercely it startled me. "Look me in the eyes and tell me that if you go our relationship will not be over. Tell me."

"I do not control the future," I said. "But if I do have to leave, I will do whatever it takes to bring you with me."

Munsi zo hanze *(abroad)*

Once I'd uttered the idea of going abroad, *munsi zo hanze*, I could not shake it off. It consumed my waking hours and my dreams. I knew I had to act. Every minute I spent working this dismal job for disappearing wages was a minute wasted, a minute longer my family quivered on the instable precipice of homelessness and poverty. I was ready to begin the process of moving to America—but I needed the blessings of my family first.

A week after Sharon's surprise visit, I made the four-hour journey to Ngoma, the village where my mother had temporarily relocated to live with my half-brother John. I rode the last hour on the back of a motorcycle taxi; the driver knew John and took me to his house withoutquestion. The trail there wove through dense jungles and marshy swamps—at one point the water was so deep we had to get off the bike and push it across.

When we arrived at the modest grass-thatched huts of my brother's property, I was exhausted in both body and mind, but my message festered inside like an old splinter wanting to get out. I hugged my siblings who ran out to greet me with distracted affection, then made a bee-line for the house. My mother met me at the door. After hugging me tightly, she pushed me back and inspected me, shaking her head and furrowing her brow.

"I will make you food," Mama offered. "You seem famished."

"No, I can wait for dinner," I said.

"You look so malnourished" she insisted.

"I'm fine, Mama."

"Let me guess. You have been stressed and are not eating well, right?" she asked.

"I have been worried about you," I admitted, then wrinkled my nose and added, "That, and the food in my work village is not that good."

Despite my protests, my mother prepared an early dinner. I hesitated to burden her mind while she cooked, and to keep from buzzing around her like a fly, I spent the time inspecting my half-brother's land and herd. When we finally sat down to plates of cassava and fried beans, my stomach churned so much with nervousness that I could barely touch the delicious food. I pecked at it, but my throat closed when I tried to swallow. I couldn't put it off any longer.

"I'm planning to quit my job, Mama," I declared. My mother's head jerked up from her plate like an antelope sensing a predator. Somberness set in among my siblings and cousins. Outside, the chirping of the crickets became very loud.

"Are you crazy?" she asked. "You have been lucky to find a government job that pays well and you are already thinking of dropping it?"

"Yes, Mama, but--."

"But what? So what are you going to do? No, what are *we* going to do?"

Her lips quivered; her voice had taken on a desperate pitch.

"I have a plan but it's only tentative," I said calmly.

"Trust me," I continued, looking around at the silent faces studying me. "I'm nervous, too. That is why I haven't resigned yet."

Robinah drummed her plastic cup with a fork. "So, what is this plan you have? You are killing us with the suspense."

I took a deep breath. "I want to go to the United States of America."

"What?" Mama inquired. "Do you even know anyone there?"

"Not really," I answered. "But I have found a potential host family. I'm hoping to be in contact with them soon."

"Obviously 'host' doesn't mean 'adopt,' " Mama challenged. "What will you do when they are done hosting you?"

"My hope is to find a job and be able to support myself—and you."

"I've heard America is the hardest country to secure a visa for," Robinah speculated. "Have you thought about Britain or Sweden?"

"Yes," I replied. "But if I am going to take this risk--I want to aim for the best."

"Did you say 'best'?" Mama asked. "Best in what?"

"C'mon, Mama," my little brother David interrupted. "You've heard on the radio, they are a superpower! They chased Sadam Hussein's army from Kuwait within a day."

I rolled my eyes at my brother. "That is not why I've chosen America. I'm going there because it is a land of great opportunity--where my skills will be in demand and I can earn a better living for all of us. A much better living."

There was a pall of silence. My siblings glanced at each other, while mother sat brooding. Then, Annet hopped to her feet. "Hooray!" she shouted. "Let's do it!" She wiggled her hips in a celebratory dance, setting off all the others to giggle. A bit of the nervousness dissipated in the air, but my mother was still tense.

"Annet, please stop," Mama ordered. "I'm worried for Patrick. Going far, beyond the oceans, without any friends or relatives there?" She got up, gathered our plates, and piled them on a tray. "So what does it take to travel to the USA?"

"A visa, a host family, an internship . . ." I answered. "And a plane ticket."

*   *   *

The next several weeks were a whirlwind of activity. Beth Hammond, a student from Tufts University who'd come to Makerere to study wildlife while I was in my final year of veterinary school, secured me a hosting arrangement with her family in rural Kentucky. Once I knew where I'd be staying, I found an internship with a veterinary clinic there. With these arrangements in place, I received my visa for travel. Once it was issued, I had three weeks to catch a flight out of the country. A local travel agent found me a ticket for thirteen hundred dollars—by far the largest amount of money I'd ever spent on a single purchase. I cashed in my savings, sold all my belongings down to the cup I drank from and the mattress I slept on, and then went around to all of my relatives, gathering what little they had to loan me. My mother sold two of her last three cows to provide the final dollars. Everything came together, not without struggle, but as if it were meant to be.

I had one final visit to make before I left.

I found Baaba sitting alone outside a half-finished hut, much like the one my father and I had slept in while watering our cows at the Nile. He leaned his old, frail body against the wall, gazing out across the small jungle-bound clearing with sightless eyes. Nearby, a flimsy make-shift fence contained his small herd. The strong smell of cow dung curdled the air.

My grandfather did not notice my approach. When I greeted him from a few feet away, he answered, "Who's there?" and immediately began struggling to pull himself up.

"It is me, Patrick," I answered, stepping forward to help him.

"Rwabagabo!" Baaba grunted. "You came to thisforest to find me?"

"Of course, Baaba. How are you?"

"As you can see, I have become useless, in fact, a

burden to Kafuuko," Baaba replied, his voice low and gravely slow with sadness.

"Don't say that, Baaba; you are breaking my heart. You'll never be a burden."

"Ah, Rwabagabo. Do you see where we are? Homeless, again. Living in a lean-to on government-owned land. And there is nothing I can do, no way I can be of help to my family anymore. I am just another mouth to feed, while they can barely feed themselves."

"Baaba, you have taken care of us all your life. It is our turn to take care of you." I told him about my plan to go to America. As I explained the winding path towards my dream of supporting him and the rest of the family-- something I was able to dream only because of his unwavering and lifelong support of my education—Uncle Kafuuko and his wife and children wandered over to listen. They stood silently behind Baaba, and I saw a bit of hope ease the lines of stress on their faces as I spoke of earning money to buy the family land and homes.

"You have my blessings, Rwabagabo," Baaba said when I was finished.

"I feel terrible to leave you. I don't know how long it will be until I can return."

"Don't worry about me; I will be okay here with your uncle." Baaba smiled again and took my hand between his leathery palms, soft and smooth and loose with age.

"It is good that you are taking this adventure. I came to this country from Rwanda for the same reasons—so I could better provide for my family. You are my Rwabagabo—always a fighter, always courageous. But I don't think I will see you again."

"Don't say that Baaba," I begged. Tears threatened the corners of my eyes. I turned away so that his blind eyes would not see them, but his hand tightened around mine and I knew that it made no difference.

"Ah Rwabagabo, it's alright. Death is part of life. The old make way for the young. It brings me peace knowing you are taking care of our family. Go to America, and don't let leaving me weigh heavy on you. You've got my blood, and you'll carry that with you always. I am proud of you, Rwabagabo."

*   *   *

On the gray afternoon of April 23, 2000, Sharon helped me pack. It didn't take long. I'd sold nearly everything I owned. With slow care, she folded the few clothes I had left and placed them in my old suitcase. The rest of my belongings--my passport, Frederick Forsyth's novel*The Day of the Jackal*, a ballpoint pen and blue notepad with my contact's phone numbers, a toothbrush, and photos of Baaba, Sharon, and my family—I placed in a small handbag.

Sharon and my half-brother John accompanied me on the slow taxi ride to the Kampala airport. For a while, we sat silent, Sharon and I facing each other across the ratty bench seats. It seemed impossible that we could have made it here; the reality of my leaving weighed heavier than my old suit case ever could. At one point Sharon reached into my handbag, removing the notepad.

"I'm getting really sad," she wrote, passing the note to me discreetly. John gazed out the window at the passing world, oblivious.

"It'll be ok," I wrote back.

She took the notebook again, tears fighting to escape the corners of her eyes. Pressure swelled my chest, a dull ache in my sternum. The miles that would soon separate us seemed as impossible as the unfathomable time that would come with them.

"I'm afraid I'll never see you again," she wrote. I gripped the pad, bending its floppy cover. All my life, I'd lived in small communities where everyone knows your name, your family, your business. When I'd been kidnapped by the bicycle thief, my father had found out within hours and set out to find me. Even when I'd snuck away to join the NRA, telling no one, my mother had quickly figured out my whereabouts and stormed the base looking for me. In my quest to find security for my family, I needed to sacrifice my own; every tendril I had ever known—that of family, friends, community, and girlfriend. If I was hungry in America, there would be no one there to feed me milk from their cow. If I needed shelter, there would be no grass-thatched huts along the river. And if I were lost, no wise old voice would help me find my way. In America I could disappear and no one would ever know.

"I'll do whatever it takes," I wrote, handing it back with shaking hands. Just then, John looked over with a smirk, and our final moments of intimacy ended as I tucked away the pad with a flush of embarrassment. Sharon wiped the tears from her face and turned back towards the window, watching the passing slums outside fading into the blur of movement.

Annet and my uncle Bangirana met us at the airport for final goodbyes. Sadness and excitement sparked the thick air as we hugged. I kissed Sharon last, holding her close to whisper, "I promise you, I will come back and get you." She didn't bother to wipe the tears from her face, but smiled through them.

As my plane taxied out towards the runway, I saw them watching from the airport's rooftop deck, waving. I waved back, unsure of whether they could see me through the window of the huge 747, but not caring either way. Face pressed to the window, I watched them fade into the distance, the past, praying that I'd made the right decision, praying that I'd see them again. Soon, there was a great surge of energy beneath me, and the jet took off. Below, the cities of Uganda become tiny smudges in a sea of green. I couldn't pull my eyes form the window, from how tiny the world looked below. The tinier the trees, hills and lakes became, the smaller I felt, alone on this thin metal craft hurtling through the sky, headed into an unknown world and an unknown future. When darkness engulfed the earth, I saw my face reflected in the glass, but it was no longer the face of a little boy. It was the face of a man, ready to take whatever risks necessary to support his loved ones. It was the face of a man who, against all odds, had become the first in his family to earn a college degree, a man who, in the midst of poverty, had secured a visa, a plane ticket, a place to stay, and a job in America--the land of opportunity. I'd made it this far. The path ahead did not promise to be any easier. But I would keep on fighting.

Afterword

April, 2013

Gutaha (The return home)

As soon as I stepped out of the plane, a thick fragrant African breeze welcomed me. I took a deep breath. Though I hadn't breathed African air in ten years, it tasted familiar. Sharon descended the metal stairway behind me, flanked by our two sons, Aaron and Ian. For a second we stood as a family, looking out at the lush green world beyond the tarmac.

"Are you Patrick Kalenzi?"

A neatly dressed young woman peered up at me.

"Yes, I am," I replied calmly, pushing revere asideto try to place her. She did not look familiar. "What can I do for you?"

"I am a colleague of your brother-in-law, Francis, and I work with government security at the airport. He asked that I take good care of you."

Within minutes, uniformed security personnel were loading our ten bags—filled mostly with gifts—onto carts. The young woman escorted us through customs to where a crowd of some seventeen relatives stood buzzing with excitement. We'd barely made it past the import customs check point when Sharon's family and my family pounced on us with warm embraces. Aaron and Ian were passed lovingly between their aunties and uncles--my little sisters and brothers, transformed into women and men.

Unlike my siblings, my mother seemed not to have changed a bit. Sixty years old, she gripped me with arms as strong as ever, that wide smile shone upon the elegant lines of her face. When she was finally able to release me, she exclaimed, "Well, well, how big you have become!"

"In America I eat five times more than you used to

feed us," I joked, causing laughter to ripple through the group.

I looked out at the new faces of my growing family. My little brothers and sisters now had children in tow. Sharon's relatives and mine, once separated by class, mingled as kin. I missed only my departed father and Baaba, but I could feel them peering down at us from above. I knew that this grand homecoming would make them proud.

Finally having gotten our fill of hugging, we piled into seven waiting cars and convoyed to the house we had rented in an upscale Kampala neighborhood. There, more relatives waited with pots of matooke, beef stew, and slabs of fresh-baked millet bread. The aroma of indigenous spices transported me back to the way Mama's cooking filled our little grass-thatched hut in Baale.

"I thank the almighty God for keeping my children and grandchildren safe in a foreign land," Sharon's mother prayed as we sat before the feast. "I thank you Lord for bringing them home safely ..."

Home. Nine years ago, I'd bought a 640-acre piece of farmland sight-unseen so that my family could finally have a place to call their own. Later that week, Sharon, Ian, Aaron and I headed out to see our land for the first time.

The property came into view with fields spread lush and green, arching trees with friendly shadows at their edges, rising back into mighty forests. We pulled up to two cinderblock buildings. I hopped out of the car, fighting the urge to get out and hug the biggest tree I could find. Instead, I looked up and thanked God silently. This was indeed my home, our home. Its fertile fields would feed my family and their herds, its rivers would slake their thirst, its towering trees and sprawling acres would forever provide protection and sanctuary for any kin in need. A flock of birds burst across the sky above me, filling it with song and brilliant color. God saying, "Welcome home."

My mother appeared in the doorway of one of the buildings—the four-room house that I'd had built for her. That smile still spread beautiful across her face. "See our home now?" she asked, raising her arms to take in the buildings behind her, and the land spreading as far as the eye could see.

For the next hour, she led me about the property, pointing out fence lines, the kraal, our forty heads of cattle, her twenty nine acres of farmland, and the all-season dam she'd built.

"Remember when you and your father used to spend the dry season chasing watering holes, far from home?" she asked, gesturing out at the clean, calm waters spreading out half the length of a football field. "Even in the driest of the drought seasons, no one in this neighborhood needs to do that any longer. All they need to do is come here."

"Now neighbors respect us. Relatives respect us,

even the government treats us fairly—especially now that they've decided to recognize Ugandan-born Rwandese as citizens."

My mother continued to update our family on the state of Rwandan politics as she led the tour back to her house.

"Tribalism is still a problem. Of course, most of it is politically motivated because of the nepotism in our government. It creates hatred for those that feel sidelined," she explained, showing us the bathrooms, the solar-powered lighting, the tank that collected rainwater from the gutters. She proudly pointed out which additions my money had purchased, and which were gifts from my siblings, three of whom had now completed higher education and gone on to well-paying jobs.

The dramatic shift in our family's economic status showed not just in the trappings it afforded but in my mother's words as well.

"Mama, you're so informed on politics," I said with a smile.

After a good laugh, she replied, "What do you expect if I'm surrounded by educated children and have enough time to attend all the political discussions in our village? Now come, let me show you where your brother Ronald is building me a new energy-conserving kitchen. He says I'll use just a fraction of the firewood that I do now."

When I'd left Uganda thirteen years ago, Baaba still served as the family rock, the organizer of dinners and reunions and other celebrations. Through these gathering and his generous administer of personal advice, he made sure that our traditions, morals, pride and rituals passed on through the generations. After he passed away, I knew it would be my responsibility to take on that role. As part of my return visit to Africa, I'd organized a huge family reunion to take place on our land. The crowning event of the party would be the baptism of my two sons, here, in their motherland. I knew that these actions would make Baaba proud.

The day before the festivities and baptism, local villagers poured in to help with the preparations. Some hauled drinking water, others prepared to slaughter a cow for the feast. By midday, out-of-town relatives and their friends began to arrive. I greeted each of them as I continued to direct the planning and preparations. The cooks trickled in, rented tents and speakers were set up, and music soon filled the air. There was no holding back the party until its scheduled beginning.

The next morning we had a quick breakfast, then headed to Migera church of Uganda. Ian and Aaron looked sharp in their white suits, and it filled me with nostalgia to see Sharon so elegant and beautiful in the long, flowing purple fabrics of a traditional Tutsi dress.

As when we had left the airport, our family arrived at the church in an entourage of cars. Our relative and friends overflowed the two-hundred-person capacity building, falling into a buzzing and happy quiet as the service began with a family-wide blessing. Soon, the pastor called for Ian and Aaron's godparents to bring them forward. He doused them with water and traced crosses over their foreheads, eliciting giggles that fell quickly to cheering that filled the building. Sharon and I looked at each other, not needing words to communicate. The joy of being surrounded by family in a place of worship, while our sons were brought into their religion in this humble church of our homeland, was simply incomparable.

We arrived back home to a party that would last for days. Music rumbled from the DJ tent, and the beer had begun to flow. By the time we'd begun serving dinner, over four hundred friends and relatives had arrived. Occasional speeches of gratitude interrupted the dancing and drinking.

"Who knew that one day, all these people, who once never knew who we were, or how we lived, would ever take the time, trek the distance, and come here to celebrate with us," my mother said to me at one point during the night. Tears wetted her eyes. "God is good!" she exclaimed, wiping them away with the back of her hand.

"God is good," I concurred. "Do you think Baaba and Dada are watching over us?"

"I believe they are. And they must be pleased with you, Rwabagabo."

Rwabagabo. It had been a long time since anyone had called me that. A lump filled my throat. I ducked my head and walked away from Mama before my own tears flowed, hoping to find a corner of privacy to collect my thoughts.

Just then a hand gently caught my elbow. I turned to see my wife. "Patrick, where are you going? It's time to cut the cake."

She met my wet eyes with a smile. Taking a deep breath, I followed her to the stage. We held our sons' hands while they cut slices through the sheets of decadently frosted butter cake and served them to the crowd. When the line finally came to an end, I took my boys to a side of the stage, gathered them in front of me, and looked out with them at the dancing crowd.

"Aaron, Ian." I spoke their names lovingly, and each looked at me with a serious gaze. I knew that I had their full attention. "Look around. These are all your people. They love you. Always remember to respect and love them back no matter how they look or what they have or don't have." I hugged them close as they stood silently watching, taking in their family, their future, and the first tendrils of a responsibility that they would someday carry. In a few days, we'd head back to America, but the sense of heritage and pride I'd passed on to them, which Baaba once passed on to me, would live on.

Acknowledgements

To my beautiful family: Sharon, Aaron and Ian, who contributed immensely and prayed for the book.

ToJeffry Weiss, Jean and David Hardwicke, Beret Strong, Chris Parks, Marlene and Ralph Ritter, my gratitude for helping me shape this book is as abundant as your assistance. And to my friend and talented writer, Aliser Geiser, who brought this book to life, I thank you all.

Follow up

For more books from the author please visit

www. patrickkalenzi.com

If you are inspired and would like to help, we suggest you find any struggling group of children in your neighborhood, country or ask us where help is needed by sending us a message on ***www.patrickkalenzi.com***.

Made in the USA
Coppell, TX
28 October 2023

23512057R00288